NINJA CHICK

NINJA CHICK

SIX SACRED LESSONS FOR BECOMING CHEEKY, IN CHARGE, AND SIMPLY GENIUS!

MOLLIE CULLIGAN

NEW AMERICAN LIBRARY

NEW AMERICAN LIBRARY
Published by New American Library, a division of
Penguin Group (USA) Inc., 375 Hudson Street,
New York, New York 10014, USA
Penguin Group (Canada), 90 Eglinton Avenue East, Suite 700, Toronto,
Ontario M4P 2Y3, Canada (a division of Pearson Penguin Canada Inc.)
Penguin Books Ltd., 80 Strand, London WC2R 0RL, England
Penguin Ireland, 25 St. Stephen's Green, Dublin 2,
Ireland (a division of Penguin Books Ltd.)
Penguin Group (Australia), 250 Camberwell Road, Camberwell, Victoria 3124,
Australia (a division of Pearson Australia Group Pty. Ltd.)
Penguin Books India Pvt. Ltd., 11 Community Centre, Panchsheel Park,
New Delhi - 110 017, India
Penguin Group (NZ), 67 Apollo Drive, Rosedale, North Shore,
Auckland 1311, New Zealand (a division of Pearson New Zealand Ltd.)
Penguin Books (South Africa) (Pty.) Ltd., 24 Sturdee Avenue,
Rosebank, Johannesburg 2196, South Africa

Penguin Books Ltd., Registered Offices:
80 Strand, London WC2R 0RL, England

First published by New American Library,
a division of Penguin Group (USA) Inc.

First Printing, May 2007
1 3 5 7 9 10 8 6 4 2

REGISTERED TRADEMARK—MARCA REGISTRADA
LIBRARY OF CONGRESS CATALOGING-IN-PUBLICATION DATA
Culligan, Mollie.
Ninja chick : six sacred lessons for becoming cheeky, in-charge, and simply genius! / Mollie Culligan.
p. cm.
ISBN-13: 978-0-451-22117-9
ISBN-10: 0-451-22117-6
1. Women—Psychology. 2. Self-realization in women. I. Title.
HQ1206.C83 2007
158.082—dc22   2006034222

Set in Filosofia
Designed by BTDnyc
Illustrations by Nils Jawa
Printed in the United States of America

PUBLISHER'S NOTE
The publisher does not have any control over and does not assume any responsibility for author or third-party Web sites or their content.

To all the NINJA CHICKS
who are just brassy enough
to say yes to a life
of perpetual riot

THANK YOU...

To my agent, Jill Grinberg, who is a
woman of incredible integrity.
In your company I have always
felt pregnant with value, to
which I've kept wondering,
"Is she mad?" You've been the tactful guide who has
navigated my shy core and my tousled, brimming
passion with a sense of real focus and drive.
To all my ninjas who have done late-night, last-minute and
long reads (Nikki, Megan my sister, Cat, Aunt Cathy,
Aunt Barb, Karine, among others).
To Sarah Manges, Megan Regard and Nils Jawa for your
commitment and your talent.
To all my cousin-sisters and aunts, to my girl Lucy, Poon-to-
the-Moon and Gramma, and to our fast ride through
the retirement community.
To all my ninjas who brought me dinner during visiting
hours while I've worked away. To those who've endured

learning curves with me over the years and have kept choosing the ride. To my Lizard, who has softened this tough girl.

To those who have taught me: Eve Ray and Paul Eaglebear.

To those who have inspired me: Dan Millman, Twyla Tharp, Julia Cameron and Anaïs Nin.

To those who have supported me: Jen Egan, David Elliot, DJ, my whole family and my extraordinary team over at the Jack Rabbit Collection.

To my Mom and Dad, who are two very interesting, dynamic human beings who have gotten behind all of my adventures and introduced me to my independence.

To my brother for your love and support and to a lifelong game of bla and Finker play.

To Anne Bohner, Claire Zion and the whole NAL team for *seeing* this book before a word was even written. To your conference table of women who met with me that day and showed me what a ninja was. Thank you for the vision and true backing. It has been a writer's dream come true.

CONTENTS

NINJA CHICK

INTRODUCTION

TALE OF THE MASTER MAMA NINJA

Deep in a lush jungle of life, past a bushel of perennial boyfriends gone very wrong, just beyond the hangover hills, and to the left of the thick briar of bounced checks, lies a sacred dojo. A place of wisdom, a place of eternal learning, a space where courageous ninjas have trained for generations. Nestled in this heart of the dojo lives Mama Ninja, our wise, magisterial guide. She is the thread that connects all ninjas; she lives inside each of us. She's the attentive voice, waiting patiently, answering kindly, inspiring nothing short of *an inner revolution*. She is ready for you to call upon her, ready to teach you the six sacred, ancient precepts that will enable you to become a ninja; to invoke your most evolved, *potent* self.

WELCOME NINJA

Congratulations on discovering the sacred six teachings. You are now invited to walk into your forest, into your dojo, take the following precepts, and emerge forever changed, forever a member of this crème de la courageous, clever, captivating, secret society of ninjas. Like a karate kid earning her black belt, you will "take" each precept by doing the various tests, tasks, and skill sets at the end of each teaching so you too can emerge a true ninja. This journey is a process. It is about being human. About being beautifully imperfect. About being ninja.

Ninja, a breed that lets the milk spill, the eggs break and the truth erupt. A breed that looks challenge right in the eye and asks her to *dance*. A breed that, simply put, is a member of the most select, fierce, and damn fine sisterhood to date.

Welcome to your tribe. Welcome to your adventure.

NINJA OATH OF HONOR

I hereby serenely swear to remember that I am never alone. I am a part of a tribe—a simply genius tribe.

I hereby sweetly swear to seek the most expansive answer to all of my challenges.

I hereby sincerely swear to take the road most rambunctious.

I hereby solemnly swear to be a good wingwoman to my fellow ninjas. I swear to talk up my ninja sister in the presence of the cute guy she's sweet on. Additionally, I will talk up my ninja in the presence of businesspeople important to her.

I pledge to uphold the precepts, guard them well and pass them on to other ninjas in waiting.

NINJA SPEAK

A ninja can be in a crowd of a hundred and understood only by her accomplice with the aid of "Ninja Speak," like a secret language for warrior ears only.

Heard Around the Dojo: On Dating

Benny—a "friend with benefits." Ex: "Yes, of course I'm stopping by my *benny* tonight. I've been extremely *dehydrated* as of late."

Bonsai—a man who needs a lot of trimming, teaching, working on. Ex: "He certainly is hot, but man what a *bonsai*! I just don't have that kind of time."

Crushed Out—feeling so crushed on a guy that the world most certainly can't go on. Ex: "I'm so *crushed out*, I can't even eat."

Dehydrated—a "dry spell," a bad streak of sexless life. Ex: "It's been seven months. I'm incredibly *dehydrated*. I'm almost ready to call last year's *benny*."

Flaccid—a man who takes the run of the mill "emotionally unavailable" to an award-winning status. The kind who picks up a woman and sleeps with her, but fails to mention his marriage, his mistress, his two children, or his vasectomy. Ex: "She went all *samurai* on him when she found out he was yet another *flaccid*."

Haiku—like the short poem that is its namesake, a haiku is a relationship that is short-lived, never understood and sorta irritating. Ex: "Oh yes, Sean? Yes, some *haikus* are better left forgotten. I pray daily for total amnesia of that entire episode."

Planting—getting your friend physically close to the person she wants to talk to; usually takes place in a social setting. Ex: "She owes me big, I practically *planted* her on his lap. Then I chatted up his incredibly challenged friend so they could have some one-on-one."

Potentials—the category of men who one would consider frolicking with. Ex: "Stop by the party, there will be a bunch of *potentials* in attendance."

Sterile—An impeccably boring guy, a ninja most likely dates him because she wants her hair played with that week by someone inoffensive. Usually dropped in under a month, unless the sterile has a *sumo*. Ex: "I just need *a good sterile* around while I'm in the last stretch of my deadline."

Sumo—a man with very gifted proportions. We do hope you have plenty of your own examples to reference here.

Wasabi—hot and spicy man. Ex: "I don't care if he does carry a man-purse, he's totally *wasabi*!"

Heard Around the Dojo: On Life in General

Going Samurai—losing your noodles on someone, going crazy. Ex: "When she found out Mark, who had only worked there for a week, got the promotion instead of her, she went all *samurai* on HR. By five the same day she had the corner office, was named head of the department and had a big smile on her face."

Roundhoused—getting blindsided by an unfortunate situation in life. Ex: "I got *roundhoused*, man. I was told I have to work the whole holiday weekend!"

Sticky—suddenly finding yourself in a very peculiar social circumstance. Ex: "When my ex walked into the bar with my old roommate it was immediately *sticky*."

Zen—being very calm about a particular situation. Ex: "She's so *Zen*. I'd be falling out of my mind."

WHAT KIND OF NINJA ARE YOU?

Choose the answer that best fits you.

1. *If someone in front of you in line for coffee is picking his nose, do you . . .*
   a. Stare at him with crazy eyes until he stops
   b. Find it to be so funny you nearly lose your place in line suppressing your convulsive laughter
   c. Give him a tissue to assist in the excavation
   d. Who cares if he's picking his nose? Your own nose happens to be too far in a book, a magazine, or lost in thought for you to even notice

2. *Sunday morning you can be found . . .*
   a. Up early—you worked out, ran a few errands and are off to meet friends
   b. Turning over to see last night's nibble still in his briefs, a bottle of wine nearby . . . empty . . . and the clock that keeps flashing twelve noon
   c. You are helping your friend move or stopping by some baby shower
   d. You are listening to chill-out tunes, sipping coffee and about to read the paper

3. *You value most in life . . .*
   a. Accomplishment
   b. Enjoyment
   c. Kindness
   d. Intellect

4. *Your favorite ninja is in a "phase" and decides to dye her hair fuchsia. You . . .*
   a. Obsess on how she's doing the wrong thing and won't get ahead in her career like that
   b. Join her and streak a few chunks of your own hair
   c. Help her do it
   d. You couldn't care less

5. *If you found a thousand dollars in an envelope on the sidewalk you would . . .*
   a. Take the money and invest in one of your many projects
   b. Spend it immediately
   c. First you try to find the owner of the money, then you give it to your friend since her car just broke down
   d. You save it for your next trip to the bookstore or for traveling you've planned on for a while

IF YOU HAD AT LEAST THREE As YOU ARE:

Obsessive-Compulsive Ninja.

You are extroverted, most likely a leader, and obsessive enough to stay up all night working on projects. You potentially can tear a situation to shreds by overthinking it, yet, on the flip side, anything you put your mind to has a vast amount of momentum  and life. Steer clear of gambling, excessive intoxications of the liquid or opposite-sexed kind and you will be fine. Nearly all great artists and geniuses tend to also be obsessive-compulsive ninjas. Focus your energy and your life will be an explosion of success.

IF YOU HAD AT LEAST THREE Bs:

Record Store Ninja.

You have the devil in you and you don't particularly care who knows it. You are disco-dancing through the record store of life, enjoying it for all it's worth; usually in the moment, generally extroverted. You have an

appreciation for happy hour, vintage clothes and invitations backstage. Stay away from credit card applications, Vegas and video cameras. Choose a creative career path that harnesses this élan vital and you will easily blossom and live a long life full of good times.

IF YOU HAD AT LEAST THREE Cs:

Mother Teresa Ninja.

You give to others first, which is commendable, but there is a strong possibility that you could use some Al-Anon. You are an idealist, hopeful, cheerful and are very enjoyable to be  around. You are thoughtful and most likely introverted. Stay away from the second cousin who is perpetually traveling, jobless, burns a lot of Nag Champa and wants to couch it for "just a month." Mother Teresa Ninjas have a great capacity for patience, and make talented instructors, writers and artists. Learn to speak up for yourself, take time for you and continue to be the reason the world heals ounce by ounce.

IF YOU HAD AT LEAST THREE Ds:

Sexy Librarian Ninja.

You prefer to stay in and read a book. You are intelligent, independent and most likely introverted. You are a distinct individual with lots of opinions who prefers to keep them all to yourself. You appreciate lots of space and would sooner die than sign up for some perky group cruise to Cabo. Challenges to a Sexy Librarian Ninja include hermit-style solitude, bad danc-ing and smarts that intimidate others into silence or reverence. Sexy Librarian Ninjas make perfect international spies, masters of finance and geek-chic scientists who stumble upon cures that save the world while making themselves a pretty mint. Learn to comfortably dip into society at regularly scheduled intervals and, with your smarts, you will be unstoppable.

IF YOU HAD A VARIETY PACK OF A, B, C, D, THEN YOU ARE:

Complex Ninja.

Simply indefinable!

HOW TO APPROACH THE SACRED SIX

Make a commitment to yourself. Understand that the enrichment of the self is of vital importance; from the center of you everything else spins out . . . love life, career, productivity, family. On the flight of life you must put on your oxygen mask first before you can help another. Set up a timeline: do a precept a month, or one a week, or just a few pages a day. This is for your growth, for your passing into ninjahood.

IT IS HELPFUL IF you pick a partner in crime or a minicrew to do the activities with. Journey together. Ninjas practice well in dojos.

Just begin. A mountain can only be climbed by taking the first step. Fall. Fail. Stumble, bumble, step ahead. Allow your process in becoming a ninja to be imperfect, humorous, real. It's only with the graduation from all six lessons that the real transformation occurs. So stick with your climb. Let's begin. Enter the ninja!

LESSON ONE:
LOVE

AT THE TRAILHEAD OF YOUR PATH TO NINJAHOOD
THERE IS A SIGNPOST WITH ONE WORD, "LOVE." IT'S
THE FIRST STOP ON YOUR EXPEDITION, THE BUILD-
ING BLOCKS FOR ALL LESSONS THAT FOLLOW.
FOR FLIGHT, EXPANSION, ERUPTION, IGNITION
AND SUCCESS; FIRST COMES LOVE.

CHAPTER ONE: WHOLE BEAN LOVE

*T*he other morning I awoke to the joyful sound of the soft patter of rain on my skylight. As I nuzzled the warm covers and got ready to throw down some snooze-button love I thought, "Um, what in hell am I supposed to be doing today? Oh-my-god-therapy-started-so-five-minutes-ago! Therapy: expensive! Therapy: can't reschedule!" I stumbled down the stairs, incurring multiple wounds to my shins, as it dawned on me. "Wait! It's raining! It never rains in LA. The back door . . . the exposed power cord . . . my roommate's incredibly expensive chair that I left out on the patio!" As I hustled to make nice with her waterlogged chair I felt something funny ruining my brand-new shorts. My once-monthly had decided that there was absolutely no better time than right that moment to surge forth and say, "Hey, man, just wanted to stop by and say hi." As I wobbled to the bathroom I thought, "What is wrong with me? Is everyone else on earth struck with this level of self-inflicted insanity? If there were a title for my existence, *clearly* it would be *My Life: Lead Inappropriately*."

I'VE BEEN ACCUSED of being "slightly disorganized," "chaotic," even "peculiarly challenged." It seems to take me longer than most humans to learn the basics, and it's taken me even longer to embrace all of my shortcomings and mis-adventures of the painful kind. In fact, it's taken me several decades to realize that very young guys who live in other countries far, far away do not qualify as candidates for lasting relationships and long-term love. It's taking me longer still to embrace my body in the "as is" flesh instead of the "after the master cleanse," "post-Atkins" or "fresh from a full body peel." Peeled, cleansed and proteined-out, with boyfriends in many major cities far, far away, I'm left with a question mark above my head when it comes to the real self-love. The stuff all the talk shows, magazines and self-helpers expound upon in between commercial breaks selling me well-packaged promises for face, bum and whole body.

HAVE YOU EVER MET a woman who you just know is brimming with a real sense of self? Maybe she's not even the hottest kitten in the litter, but she definitely has something else going on, something bigger, something emanating from her. Shining. Blazing. Drawing you in. Do you notice how everyone around her is lit by her presence? Gathered round, wanting inches, energized from just an encounter. This is a ninja living from her center, regardless of the exterior. She lives from her essence. Each of us has this essence, our most true self—the unadulterated, unguarded, playful, fierce and damn fine self. Like a lil' bean resting at the pit of you, deep inside; the bean that's always been. Love the bean. Live from the bean.

Fancy that; to achieve total love of the self, the ultimate bean dream, I'm supposed to embrace the same body I refer to as traitor, defector, double agent? I'm supposed to accept every man accident I've had and every ten-thousand-dollar learning curve about the importance of refilling your engine oil? The way of the ninja is to do just that, to smile in the face of imperfection and love exactly what is, exactly how it is, in this exact moment. Put down this book. Go to a mirror, look at yourself; notice that first you might want to pick at a pimple—stop. Love the pimple. Love the woman behind the pimple. Love the entire imperfect, delectable picture now.

IN THE SHAMBHALA BOOK *The Sacred Path of the Warrior* meditation master Chogyam Trungpa talks about how each of us has essential goodness within. We are born with this vital good, and once we realize this we no longer have to convince, embellish or dress up our sense of being enough: *we already are*. All right, Trungpa, I can jive with you, meditation man. I have this basic goodness within, a good bean; I am good. I know what comes next: the watering or the starvation of my good bean. Daily bean maintenance. The goal is to increase the sheer percentage of good bean care over neglect, negative self talk, and very bad behavior. Give to yourself as freely as you would give to a friend. See your good qualities and accept your flaws as a beautiful part of being human, even if every meal you ate today just happened to be stale birthday cake that you found in the office kitchen. Even if it is four in the morning and you swore you'd never call your ex ever, ever, ever, and oh-my-god-he's-picking-up! Learn to love yourself in the raw, unconditional, profound way that you love your little sister or your best-friend-forever. Know you'll never, no matter the circumstances, leave her side for one solitary second. This is the way of the ninja, to love yourself that ceaselessly. Evolvingly. Abundantly.

THE MOST INTIMATE, sensational relationship you are capable of isn't the one with Prince Charming, even if you are beachside, a couple of glasses of sangria in hand, and he's whispering sweet Portuguese nothings in your ear. The most satisfying relationship is the one you can have with yourself—your greatest ally, advocate and friend. Ninjas, grab your beans. Let's begin!

TUMBLING TOWARD THE SELF: A WARRIOR'S GUIDE
Accept Everything Beyond the Bean

Self-love starts with self-acceptance. Loving my imperfect self is difficult enough, yet the most challenging time to shout out with love like an Up With People world tour is during a true emotional drought. It is when I'm in an inconsolably fussy mood that I add to the problem by judging my state of disarray. Then I get frustrated for judging myself, and then I judge how angry I am getting. My friend and sweat lodge leader, Paul Eaglebear, reminds me that, without ebb, we can never have flow. To develop an appreciation, and maybe even an enjoyment, of the ebb, accept the cranky dry season as easily as you flourish in the feel-good flow. Love yourself through three-thousand-dollar mistakes as easily as you do when you're on top of the world eating leafy greens. Simply, if you can love yourself when life within you feels dim, then you have a shot at loving every single gorgeous shade of gray.

Daily Bean Maintenance

Loving the bean is an active, daily choice, not a propulsion sustained lifelong from one hearty kick. Without daily water and sun, the bean wilts. You have to commit to the self, just like a partnership, and communicate with it daily. Listen well. Give well. Receive well. You can't coast off the peace you got the time you tried meditation ten years ago, ya dig? Choose one doable thing for your bean maintenance daily. Doable meaning "not rigid." If it becomes a *have to work out every day for two hours without fail,* then it's a setup *to fail.* Sneak in a workout, a writing session to free up spinning thoughts, a bath, a vase of flowers, a run. Okay, personally I don't run unless someone's chasing me, so a very fast walk.

Bean Esteem

We grow self-esteem by doing estimable acts. When you make choices, treat yourself as if you're a person of value, even on days when you don't buy it. Seems entirely elementary until

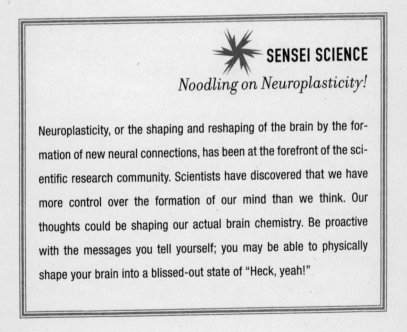

SENSEI SCIENCE

Noodling on Neuroplasticity!

Neuroplasticity, or the shaping and reshaping of the brain by the formation of new neural connections, has been at the forefront of the scientific research community. Scientists have discovered that we have more control over the formation of our mind than we think. Our thoughts could be shaping our actual brain chemistry. Be proactive with the messages you tell yourself; you may be able to physically shape your brain into a blissed-out state of "Heck, yeah!"

three Jack and Cokes in, when you're accidentally going home with a cute what's-his-name, and a cute where's-my-pants is falling far south of stated intention to take this slow. Then you lose the next day to the dire hangover and guilt. It's like playing with dominoes: you have to consciously choose each move. One choice knocks over another, and another, and then the whole getup collapses in one chaotic clatter. It's the slight navigational adjustments that keep the plane heading north. Constantly ask the question at each turnoff, "Now, Ms. Ninja, does this route leave me silly with self-esteem? Will I feel good about this tomorrow? In an hour? Am I being good to my lil' bean today?" Navigating small wins throughout the day helps you to feel so good that more healthy choices become the norm, raising the bar, the altitude at which you cruise. Eating for health, stating your truth in a work situation, asking for what you want in a negotiation, getting enough sleep, treating your temple well and pampering your palace with posies. Higher, higher. Ninjas are known to reach extraordinary heights.

Lessons from a Warrior

You teach others how to treat you by how you treat yourself. As humans we allow exactly the amount of not-nice from

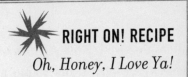

RIGHT ON! RECIPE
Oh, Honey, I Love Ya!

Sweet, delicious honey mask. Boil two cups of green tea. Sip luxuriously on one. Once the other is cooled to a nice, warm temperature, pour in a bowl and splash on the face while saying, "Honey, I love ya!"

In a bowl stir together:

1 tablespoon warm honey
1 tablespoon green clay
(if not available substitute 100%
natural colloidal oatmeal)
1 tablespoon aloe vera gel

Apply to face in upward circular motions while meditating on three reasons you like your bean.
Leave on for 15 min.

Green tea is rich in antioxidants that slow down aging, fight viruses, reduce high blood pressure, and lower blood sugar and cholesterol. It is said to fight cancer and boost the immune system. It's great both externally and internally.

others that we inflict upon ourselves. Any more and you say, "Wait—this person can't treat me like that; even *I* don't talk to myself like that." Anyone is welcome to walk all over you within the same range that you do. It's like living in a constant pigsty laced with month-old dirty dishes, but expecting guests to pick up after themselves. Essentially, if you talk to yourself like a trucker on a five-day amphetamine run, then you can expect the same from others. Speak to yourself kindly, gently, teaching by example. Know yourself. Know your value. Know your worth. Own it, and watch as others do, too.

IT IS THE PRIMARY DISCIPLINE of the ninja to raise the collective light and love in the world by first cooking it well-done within yourself. The word for self-confidence in Tibet is ziji. "Zi" meaning "shine" and "ji" meaning "splendor or dignity." Be the bean. Live from your bean and let your splendor shimmer and shine. Happiness doesn't knock *on* your door once you've finally become perfect. Happiness knocks *down* your door once you realize that you already are.

DOJO ON THE GO-GO
Falling in Love with Ebb

Practice falling in love with the ebb. For one week be conscious of the crabby days, the canceled plans, the double latte tanked across your new peacoat while you were attempting to jar open the elevator. Think of the droughts, the ebbs in yo' flow. Practice not only accepting them, but finding some sort of enjoyment in them, because walking around all day with spilled coffee down your chest can be quite humorous. Truly, sad moments can be the most beautiful; without them there would be less poetry, art and Etta Jameses in the world. Challenge yourself to accept and enjoy your bad days. Let it be. Don't judge it, because on the other side there will always be flow. There is no such thing as stasis; every moment is unique, the only consistency is change.

Retrain the Brain

Write yourself right! It takes twenty-one days to change a habit, so let's take the next twenty-one to do some neuroplastic reprogramming.

Wake up five to ten minutes early. Grab a piece of recycled paper and a thesaurus. If you are feeling a certain negative way, then write one word that is the exact opposite. Look up that word in the thesaurus, and jot down the most power-ful words noted. Write these words in a proactive sentence: "I am full of vigor. I am energetic. I am an awfully lively ninja."

Then write two examples of a time in your life when you embodied that quality. Remember it in the thick of every synapse in your brain. Afterward, for real kicks, fold up each day's note and hide it somewhere you can mysteriously stum-ble across it later. For me, this is easy. My life is so chaotic I can barely find my keys, much less a ninja note. Depending on your recall abilities you may need a neighbor or friend to hide the notes for you. It's also a guaranteed good time when guests stumble upon them.

Big Bean Love

Go out and purchase plant or herb seeds that can easily sur-vive in the climate you live in. Get a cool container (a metal bucket, mod plastic container, big, vintage jelly jar) and fill it halfway with rich soil. Brace yourself for some dork time and then write down on little pieces of paper things you want to work on, to germinate within yourself. Plant them in the soil with the seeds. Fill the rest of the container with soil. To make your seedlings grow, you need to nourish them consis-

tently. Each day when you take time to care for the plant, rit-
ualistically take those moments to think of your intentions
and what specific ways you can nourish them today. It's so
much easier to manifest that for which we have a vision. How
can we create something we can't even see?

CHAPTER TWO: FAMILY

I had the typical, run-of-the-mill, dysfunctional family of the peculiar and slightly eccentric kind growing up. It was "character building." An Irish-German lot with a taste for booze and a mind for stubbornness, we lived in a smaller suburban area with a flare for similarity, symmetry and organization. My family was anything but. First of all, we had chickens. Who among a row of picket fences and mowed lawns has a pseudoranch in their backyard with unwieldy Rhode Island Reds and a set of no-respect-for-sleeping-in, crowing crew of roosters? It was always a good time when a few of them would get loose and we'd have to chase them down asphalted streets like farm-kid lunatics. (No offense to farmers.) I'm sure we were quite the vision, which wasn't helped along one night when my mom and I had a makeshift midnight parade. I happened to be upset about something and, to cheer me up, my mom insisted we throw on layers of goofy dress-up clothes topped off with winter jackets, house robes and ski goggles: then we marched through the neighborhood singing "You and I travel to the beat of a different drum." Just Mom, myself, Linda Ronstadt and the neighborhood in awe. During the holidays, instead of a normal family vacation oohing and aahing at the Grand Canyon or lying supine poolside at the Radisson on the Big Island, we jeeped through the jungle interior of Belize, windows down, skin crusted over in road dust. We rolled up one night to some tiny Garifuna village without hotel reservations, or even any vague notion that there would be any form of tourist housing besides bribing some local family for a couch. We got out of the car just as everyone from the village was coming together for a ritual gathering for what we were to find out later was a dance symbolic of their days of slavery. Did I mention we are a stark, chalky, untannable white folk? Lucky for us it didn't matter. Soon enough I had someone's baby, with stunning purple eyes, in my arms and the community enveloped us in their carefree night. My upbringing wasn't typical, but it sure was educational. From a bland town, born of a slightly insane family and incubated with a big sense of adventure, I craved the wanderlust and independence I had been taught so I left my hometown the first chance I could. As the saying goes, "you can't choose your family, but you can choose to move a million miles away from them."

MILES AWAY or down the block, a ninja's primary purpose is to live a life led by love: in all relations, in every decision, nearly every day; even at family reunions. The family inferno is particularly hot with opportunities to practice acceptance and love. For some of you it's probably effortless to get along with kin. I envy you. For those of us not in denial it can be a bit more . . . arduous. It's difficult to accept your mom when you leave the room for five minutes at the holidays only to overhear her showing your brand-new boyfriend your chub-ster elementary school pictures from the year you had the overprocessed perm, with Mom falling just short of cracking open the pages of your childhood diary (which she already knew by rote) while making annotated lists of its contents.

The starter step in familial recovery is to accept them just as they are. Before this genuine acceptance causes you to break out in spontaneous Pollyannish hives, you must first

After too many consecutive days logged with the family, temptations to check in to a local institution may abound. Before pulling a little *Girl, Interrupted*, try a happy family detox of mind, body and sanity.

THE HEALING HOT TURMERIC TONIC

Turmeric is known for its free-radical-fighting antioxidants and for healing familial frustrations.

Boil two cups of water, then add one teaspoon of powdered ginger and one teaspoon of powdered turmeric. Simmer for ten minutes while you do your detox deep breaths (below). Strain detoxifying tea into a mug, add one tablespoon of maple syrup (or raw molasses for extra iron, which every good ninja needs!), a squeeze of lemon, and stir. Drink while warm.

HAPPY FAMILY DETOX DEEP BREATHING

Take an extremely deep breath, and exhale with fast, staccato pulses of fire, pushing out all that you might have held in while you listened to your aunt proclaim that soon the only guys available for you to date will be a pile of bitter divorcés. While you breathe out, let go of all they are, remembering that just because you share genes doesn't mean you are clones. They get to be themselves and you get to be all you. Do this five times.

forgive. You must first wrestle with something in order to pin it down; scale the mountain in order to reach the top. To accept without true forgiveness is like forcing a clown smile over fury and calling it a fine time. With real forgiveness, acceptance just happens.

I had the good fortune of being cut open and having an organ removed to come to this thing called forgiveness. I was in the middle of the busiest time of my life, the ass-kicking start of my accessory design business, and I was about to ship my very first, hard-earned national order to Barneys while simultaneously working to secure a follow-up order. No time for a lil' vaca to the hospital for a sit-in with the family, but I didn't have much of a choice. The doctors needed to julienne my thyroid to make sure I didn't have malignant cells. I was forced to veer immediately from fast lane to dusty shoulder, impounded to a bed on my back in a small hospital room with my parents *for days on end.* I hope your road to clemency is a bit easier.

Hours after the surgery I had a bit of a panic, finally taking in the weight of what was going on. I was alone with my mom and my dad, one on each side of me, bent into my hospital bed. It was the first time the three of us had been in one room in fifteen years. My normally strong body felt cracked. I was tied to tubes, face completely white, neck immobilized, throat almost closed, unable to speak, barely able to swallow my own spit. My life went from sheer independence, running at a million miles a minute, to an abrasive stop. There, stripped of everything, in this incredible, thick silence, I looked across at the two people who dared to birth me and what I saw wasn't my parents. I saw two human beings. I saw in their eyes such terror, such raw love, and so much fear at the state I was in and what it meant. I saw two amazing, fallible, touchable, imperfect human beings who had done the best they could at the ripe age of twenty when they made the crazy decision to spawn children. And for some reason that's all it took. A flood of built-up childhood angst began to rinse away.

I had spent all this time moving on, moving away, shutting them out. Some of it was healthy; some of it was mere walls. What changed for me in that instant was that I suddenly saw those walls as optional. For the rest of the time in the hospital we all sat about together, chatting, laughing, ordering rounds of popsicles. It was easy and light and freakin' cool . . . and probably helped along by copious amounts of opiates.

Don't go waiting for forced hospitalization; start accepting now. Start forgiving now. Today. Whatever it takes. There is no better moment. We never know when any of us will be yanked from the stage, curtain drawn. If that has already happened with one of your loved ones, then you really know the weight of this. Even if a family member is no longer with you, there is still the opportunity to accept and forgive the past, even the loss. Family is not a choice; love is. The choice of the warrior? To unwaveringly choose love like it's your last day on stage.

DOJO ON THE GO-GO
Write Yourself Right!

For two pages, do some free-association writing about your core qualms regarding your family. If you need a few more pages than two, set aside the weekend and have a go at it! Afterward, take out another two pages and go on an imaginative journey. Tell the story of your parents. Dip back in time and describe where they came from, what kind of parents they had and everything they were dealing with while they were raising you. The idea is to get a better understanding of where they were coming from so that you can begin your climb toward forgiveness and total acceptance.

CHAPTER THREE: SHOSHIN

*T*here's a story about a professor who visited a monk. The monk started pouring the professor a cup of tea, and he just kept pouring and pouring, tea spilling everywhere. The guest flipped out, to which the monk explained that his mind was like the teacup; too filled with his own ideas to let anything new in. Empty your teacup so we can begin.

Let's begin. Let's get to the place we all once knew, when we were children: unscathed, open, willing, malleable, curious. Shoshin, a Japanese martial arts word, describes the state of consciousness that always remains fresh. It is a warrior's goal to live every moment with a clean-slated beginner's mind . . . even after you find out that, when he mentioned he was "duplicitous," what he meant to say was that he had a secret life involving a tall Russian the night before, two Brazilians a month back and a few female coworkers along the way. Even after the promotion you worked eighty hours a week for months to earn was given to the boss's daughter, who on day one kicked you out of your office, pinned up a rhinestone-embroidered sorority flag on what was your calendar and then spent two hours on the phone talking about where to get the best mani. Even after the friend you thought you knew "got to know" the boyfriend you'll never want to know again. Even after all forms of catastrophic hurt—after all of the "they'd nevers" are replaced by "they sure dids"—we

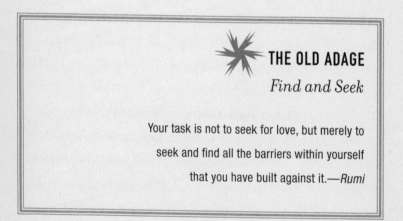

THE OLD ADAGE

Find and Seek

Your task is not to seek for love, but merely to seek and find all the barriers within yourself that you have built against it.—*Rumi*

have the choice to begin again, to act as if the skid marks burning on the heart aren't really impeding every decision, infusing every choice with a brand new sense of "oh, hell no."

The struggle for shoshin is like that of a child, once totally open to the world, who reached for the warm light of a flame only to feel the scorch on her skin. She never wants to touch again. How can you remain open and get to know a new crush when you are acutely aware of the possibility of the affair ending in a third-degree burn? I, for one, have employed great skill in avoiding personal availability to burns. I've traveled far away, worked eighty-hour weeks and cushioned myself with dozens of friends and busy schedules—leaving no room for "that." It's comfortable. It's safe. And at the end of the day all of it is just evidence of the charring around my heart, the iron guard candy-coated by names like "cool" and "indifferent," "elusive" and "tough." Remember, there is a difference between being tough and being courageous. It only takes a protective guarding to be tough, but it takes fearless courage to crack open. And it takes a warrior to remain open.

To obtain this state of shoshin you must first understand a universal fact about humans: unless someone is wack, a person's top priority is not to hurt others on purpose. The ways in which others have ended up hurting me usually speak more about their limitations, our timing, the lessons I needed to learn and general time spent in therapy. But it is not proof that the masses are out to make sure I am hurt by a thousand voodoo pins of pain. Hurt happens; it's the way we are challenged as humans to shake it up and grow. Forgive the past. Forgive the humanity in others. Put it to rest. Let it go. Empty your cup.

After forgiving all of the firestarters and emptying all of the cups in her house, a warrior must learn to use the past, as opposed to wading around in it. You don't have to think of memories as "bad" experiences or wasted time. In Zen everything has the same value. Everything is the Buddha. The Buddha exists everywhere, in every person, every experience, every lesson: good, bad or hellaciously ugly. What matters is that you are circling closer and closer toward your truth through each debacle. That is the nature of life; all of us spinning around, running into dozens of others, taking nicks and chips off each other. We chip away until what is left is a beautiful sculpture, shaped by life, shaped by our lessons. The task of the warrior is to choose opening relentlessly; to allow others to touch you, chip away at you and teach you. In this way all experiences have a home as our instructors. Use your past as the fuel for wisdom. Use the past to learn that you

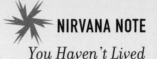

NIRVANA NOTE

You Haven't Lived
Until You've Smudged

A way to begin fresh and achieve home shoshin is to smudge! Everything that happens within your home leaves a trace: stinky feet, bad attitudes, the crabby neighbors you can hear through the walls. Smudging is a Native American tradition of lighting herbs, typically sweetgrass or sage, to clear a space of leftover energy.

Take a bundle of dried sage and light the ends of it, blow out the flame, create a nice smoke and wander around the home smudging the smoke at will. This is best if done in the nude. Or at least very amusing.

The list of smudgeables:

* Sage—the most typically used herb for purification and renewal, said to evict negative energy.
* Sweetgrass—often burned after the sage to welcome positive energy.
* Lavender—increases the peace and attracts a whole lotta love.
* Mugwort—stimulates awareness and powerful dreams.
* Rosemary—good for clarity, perplexing problems and hangovers.

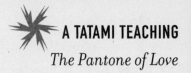

A TATAMI TEACHING
The Pantone of Love

Think of others as each being a specific color on the pantone color wheel, distinct, like the primary shade of their basic character. I might be a deep cobalt blue with a pearlescent finish. I'm attracted to strong oranges, kind lavenders, fire engine reds. Sometimes I've gotten close to a perfectly good marigold and begged them to be a shade more ruby. If only they could *just* be a bit more ruby! I've been frustrated with them over their natural shade, even taking it to the extreme of thinking, "If they loved me enough, they most certainly would shift a shade closer to scarlet . . . at the very least!" And all they're doing is being their beautiful marigold self.

Allow others to be the colors and characters they already are, honor them, be truthful about the hue you are really looking for in life and don't fall short a few shades. There is someone else out there who is starving for a perfect shade of marigold and there is someone in a perfect shade of ruby just waiting to embraced.

don't need to tumble down hills with every Jack and Jill. Get intuitively selective, make wise choices about who is worth the fall and, once you have, dive like you've never been bludgeoned before!

DOJO ON THE GO-GO
Your Partner Picker:
Pick Your Pantone and Tumble Toward Toitsu

Awareness of your patterns can help free you from them. Once free from repetitive picking, you can find out what shade you are genuinely interested in. To refine your partner picker, you must first know the patterns of your previous picking. The point is to get closer to what, in the Japanese arts, is called Kan, or intuitive perception. With awareness and intuitive perception, partner picking will be made less repetitive and insane.

TAKE FIVE PIECES OF PAPER and place them side by side in a long row.

Page one: List all your past partners.

Page two: List why past relationships didn't work out. Write down any major destructive characteristics in them or you. List what was brought out in you in the relationship.

Page three: List the way you felt about yourself in the relationship.

Page four: Write about who they reminded you of, and of the times in your life when you felt similar to the way you did in the relationship. (Usually some primal relationship: Mom, Dad, when I was ten . . .)

Page five: Make a list of all you want in another. If you are in a partnership already, clarify these qualities in that partnership, or what you want in your friends, family and business relationships.

In Japan toitsu means "unification." This precept is about the unification of the self to make a whole person, available for a great tumbling between two complete spirits. In order to achieve happy toitsu, you have to identify what color on the wheel you want. After you make your list, look it over and circle the top five qualities. Now, *be* those qualities on a daily basis! Sow in yourself that which you wish to reap, in new relationships or those you already are in. All of life is a mirror, and we attract in others exactly what we ourselves are. Work on the toitsu of the self in order to tumble happily with another.

LESSON TWO:
FLY

WITH YOUR LOVE BEAN INTACT, YOU ARE PRIME
FOR THE NEXT LESSON, NINJA CHICK. READY
YOURSELF FOR FLIGHT. FOR A BIRD TO TAKE OFF
SHE MUST FIRST LET GO OF ALL THE EXTRANEOUS
WEIGHT THAT HOLDS HER DOWN. TYPICAL HUMAN
ACCUMULATION, SOCIAL EXPECTATIONS AND
PEOPLE-PLEASING CLOG OUR NATURAL SENSES OF
INTUITION AND DIRECTION. IN THIS LESSON YOU
WILL SHED ALL VARIETIES OF INAUTHENTIC EXCESS
TO TRAVEL LIGHT, FIND YOUR TRUE NORTH AND
READY YOURSELF FOR LIVELY AVIATION.

CHAPTER FOUR: BREAKING THE TIES THAT BLIND: SHEDDING ALL THAT ISN'T YOU TO FIND OUT JUST WHAT IS

*B*y the time I was twenty-five I had stumbled into acquiring everything I assumed a human who might later be forced to attend school reunions should have. I had rustled up a tall, normal boyfriend; we saw each other on Wednesday and Saturday nights, and barbequed on the weekends. I had a job title that made my parents proud, one I liked to say out loud. I stubbornly bought the vintage sports car of my dreams, despite the whole "being able to afford it" part. I finally felt like I belonged to the world, like I was *enough*.

Then a hilarious thing happened. The guy shattered my heart the very weekend my dad flew more than a thousand miles just to meet him. The job laid me off during the great internet boom Morning After. Two weeks before the holidays. Without severance. Then, just for giggles, months later the car I had mistaken for a bullet, the six-cylinder wonder that could spoon curves and have multiple orgasms in one purring breath, pulled me over in a huff of smoke, had a cardiac arrest and died. She was ten years from being paid off. Everything I had mistaken myself for had been systematically stripped away. I was left starkly naked. With or without my permission, life had broken all my ties that blinded. Crisis! Who was I if not all these things that stamped societal approval of my existence? I certainly didn't know how to walk through the world in my own skin, alone, without those conventional accoutrements preceding me. So, like a good ninja, in my flustered, heartbroken, penniless state, I sold what was left and skipped the country within a week. Finding yourself always tastes better in foreign lands, flirting with the local fare. In addition to the maniacal fun of jetting around and incurring catastrophic amounts of debt, I had this striking opportunity to stop and come clean about what I really wanted out of this short stint on earth. I began to

RIGHT ON! RECIPE
The Tart Taste of Letting Go

A daily swig of raw, unpasteurized, organic apple cider vinegar is an incredible detoxifier, helping your body release all that is no longer conducive to health. Apple cider vinegar is one of the most powerful home remedies. It has been known to help with acne, high cholesterol, chronic fatigue and weight loss! It is thought to help balance pH levels, and it contains trace amounts of minerals, calcium, magnesium, vitamins C, E, B_1, B_2, B_6, as well as the provitamin beta-carotene. Take about two tablespoons in a glass of water three times a day. Or if you're really feeling samurai, swig it straight. Take through a straw or rinse mouth with water after to protect the enamel on your purdy ivories.

develop my own individual, human bottom line, my personal code of the ninja.

LIKE A SNOWBALL WITH A seed at its center, we roll down the Mount Fuji of life, amassing layers of expectations and misbeliefs about ourselves and how we should live our lives, until the simple seed can no longer be seen. This blind, insulating accumulation starts to seem like life stats taken at the hospital: "Yep, she bought her first condo, check! Blood pressure and career title? Check, check. Pulse and marriage certificate? Check."

As humans we sometimes tumble far from our truth. As warriors, we fight to come back. We shed every single thing standing in our way, and sometimes, when we don't, life has this lovely way of doing it for us anyway. Stop and ask yourself a few essential questions. Who am I living this life for? What ideas about myself are holding me back? Am I keeping my life small because of some misconception that I won't be liked if I'm successful? Am I afraid I won't be liked if I'm not successful enough? Am I in my career because I truly love it, or because it makes others happy, impressed or comfortable? And the real doozy for the type A ninjas: am I so ambitious and forward-moving because I desperately love what I do and just can't seem to put it down . . . or do I work and push so hard because I'm afraid I won't have enough money, success or adoration if I don't?

ARE YOU IN A JOB because it is the one that makes your parents most proud? Because you are content with how it sounds to others? Are you with a partner because it's soothing to have someone to torture at will? Afraid to move on from a situation because it would involve risk, change, uncertainty, furniture shopping? Afraid to stop eating a baker's dozen before bed because mainlining sugar is more comfortable than sitting still and being in the moment? Striving so feverishly to prove something to someone you might run into from your college past?

You must cut a few buds if you want your rosebush to grow back twice as abundant. Look at your life. Intuitively you know what is not authentically a part of you. You know what is ready to be clipped. Whether it's a relationship or a little habit, letting go of what stands between you and your most pure self can be painful and radical. We warriors are here for epiphanies and progress. To pass this essential lesson in becoming a ninja, you must identify all the ties that blind, and then let each of them go.

The warrior's way is to get in touch with the core of you, the you at the center of all that snow. The you that laughs easily and feels light and can't wait to wake up in the morning. The you that looks straight in the eyes of those you love, speaking nothing but your truth. The you that doesn't need to prove anything or live for anyone, is just enough, exactly as is. So your life rarely feels like a "have to," and nearly always feels like a "want to." A "can't *wait* to."

DOJO ON THE GO-GO
Clutter Bug Clearing

Clearing out the clutter in your space is a great physical metaphor for shedding. One time I had a friend stay at my place and, after a week, she was so appalled at what she called the "great albatross that is your closet" that she came over and enforced the clutter bug clearing exercise.

The rules:

1. Buy proper storage containers, lots of them.
2. Tear through all your "stuff." Do not take time to relish all the little bits of your past. Box and label them. It helps to have a friend with a whip nearby.

3. Keep no two things. Pack-ratting comes from a negative sense of scarcity, i.e., there won't be enough later so I had better hold on to the forty-five bars of Holiday Inn soap.
4. Keep only the very best. Only the French milled almond soap in a velvet box. You are worth the best, so keep only the best as a physical reflection of this principle.
5. If you haven't used or worn it in over a year, give it away. You clearly haven't missed it yet, or even remembered that you had it!

When you are done and your place is a space of fresh warriorship, buy a bouquet of flowers to celebrate.

Break the Ties That Blind

You've cleared your physical space. Now it's time to identify the more elusive ties that blind. Grab a piece of paper and answer the following questions off the top of your head. Omit nothing, take the time for everything.

1. What were the rules that you grew up with? What is on the list of the unforgiven? What are the choices

that, if you made them, you feel your family or circle
of support would judge heavily?

2. Would they really judge you, or is this just how *you*
   might judge yourself projected onto those around
   you? If the judgments are not projected but real, are
   they relevant anymore?

3. If they are real, and relevant to another, do they still
   have to be significant to you?

4. What did your parents encourage you to study and
   pursue in life, or tell you that you were good at?

5. What are the secret wishes that your parents had for
   their *own* lives? Did they pursue them? What did
   they do with their lives?

6. When you were very little, what were you naturally
   drawn to? What hobbies, interests and activities
   were you always curious about? What were the top-
   ics of books, TV shows or movies you were drawn
   to? Are there any themes?

7. Take a whole page for this one. If you had no financial, training or time constraints, what would you do
   with your short stay here on earth?

Untangling the Ties

Did you notice if any of the messages or rules you received when you were little affect your life today? Are you able to untangle some of those messages and see them as being no longer applicable?

Did you notice any similarity between your parents' secret dreams and their encouragement of your pursuits? Are their dreams similar to what you are doing in your life today?

Are you closer to knowing what you ache to do at your core? In Lesson Four we will explore the pursuit of what you've discovered here.

The Human Bottom Line

To graduate to the next level in your ninja training you must first develop your own individual human bottom line. The words you live by, and would die by. Sit down with pen and paper and craft your bottom line—what is most important to you, what you stand up for, what you want with this incarnation. Once you have your unshakable human bottom line, at each twist and turn in life you can ask yourself, "Does this jive with my bottom line?"

CHAPTER FIVE: YOUR TRUE NORTH

*T*ottering around in smart tuxedoed attire, emperor penguins unerringly traverse miles of treacherous, monotonous icy abyssed by instinct alone to return to their breeding ground and make whoopee. Adult salmon journey from the great expanses of the sea back to the river of their birth, sometimes to the exact same spot where they were spawned. At times they travel more than a thousand miles led by pure instinct. We humans have this same unerring instinct ready to guide us home. Instinct—that intangible "feeling" that has kept our species alive, making us hyper-aware of a predator in the forest or a path we shouldn't take—is the primal force fueling our survival. Now, with all the luxury of modernity, we are comfortably padded from this essential, primal intuition. Getting back in touch with that little nudging inside, and then standing by it with all you're worth, is a vital skill of the warrior. How often do you feel that subtle first intuition, but then are submerged beneath the cascade of reasons, opinions and excessive analysis until your simple truth becomes too diluted to see? An essential task of the warrior is to unearth your inner compass and then practice walking in the direction it points *no matter what*. It's called following your intuition toward your own personal "true north," the longitude toward your most absolute, individual truth.

I WENT THROUGH A STAGE once where I couldn't walk an inch without a dozen-person survey confirming that the step was a good one to take. I asked advisors, moms, sisters, friends, therapists, neighbors, the butcher and the mailman about every mental, emotional, relationship and business move I considered making. Some people just seem to have been spat out onto the playground knowing it all, hands shooting into the air with decisive answers. But I've always felt like I was on eternal ditch day when information was selectively dosed out. Certainly, everyone else was the expert. Even if it was our first day in class, they all *just knew*.

Seeking answers from outside yourself can be expansive and refreshing, and it can also be diluting. We are all human—therapists, doctors and mentors included. Each of us podcasts our opinions through the colored veils of our own individual experiences. If someone is on his baker's dozenth divorce, then his love advice might come in a nice shade of abysmal charcoal. Ask someone who grew up on the coast about living a high-altitude, mountainous life and you'll get her best sea-level perspective—surf tips, useless for the rocky peaks you scale. Your north is unique, particular to you alone.

Reach, connect, expand, question, read, receive; let all of that information settle into your skin, *and then go further*. Go deeper into the subterranean levels of the self and trust your own quiet answers. Practice tuning in to that voice. Practice honoring it, giving it time to speak. Practice believing in it, flying in the direction to which it nods. Absolutely

SABAKI-SPA!

My Clever Cucumber

My Clever Cucumber is a succulent, homemade face mask rich in cooling, recuperative properties.

MY CLEVER CUCUMBER

½ cup chopped cucumber

½ cup chopped avocado

1 egg white

2 tsp. powdered milk

Mush all of the ingredients in a blender until they form a smooth, pastelike consistency. Apply 2 tablespoons of My Clever Cucumber to your face and neck in circular, upward motions while imagining yourself heading toward your metaphoric true north. Leave the mask on for 30 minutes, or until dry. Rinse with warm water, followed by a cold-water rinse.

Finish by moisturizing your face with pure aloe vera gel. Aloe, said to be a favorite of Cleopatra, has been used medicinally for centuries for burns and boo-boos. It accelerates healing, and promotes new cell and tissue growth. Translation: young, dewy skin!

no one can give you the validation that you can give yourself. Drawing wise waters from your own well is an incomparably powerful, metamorphic experience. Wait for no one's opinion, no one's confirmation. With confidence in your own compass, you no longer need to justify your actions or defend yourself. That's the truth of the compass and the truth of heading north: You. Standing for yourself in the raw, sensual nudity of your certainty and saying, "*Absolutely. Hell, yes.*" The right decisions, solutions and resolutions will no longer need to be discovered . . . *they will be lived.*

DOJO ON THE GO-GO
Uncovering the Compass

Should I ditch work and run off to Vegas with some guy I just met? Should I confront this new friend about something that bothered me? When you are in the midst of indecision, madly searching your clutch for your compass to no avail, stop and ask yourself these deciphering questions:

In a year, which experience will I remember?

If I don't do it, will I think about it more than five times a day?

Will I be able to fall asleep tonight if I don't do it, or if I do it?

Which will I feel better about tomorrow? In a month? In a year?

En-Compass-ing Meditation

When you are confused about decisions, muddy with expectations or unclear on the difference between the distracting opinions of others and your own intuition, then *take flight, go north*. Sit, center and soar.

THIS AMERICAN INDIAN PRAYER AND meditation was taught to me by a Jesuit priest I met in primarily Hindu Katmandu while I was studying Tibetan Buddhism; talk about a cultural smorgasbord! It was passed down to me because I am a busy body who abhors sitting still for a two-minute tutorial on how to work my new phone, much less sitting in silent meditation for several minutes in a row. I need something chewy, more interactive than a sit-in. Try this powerful directional meditation. It roots you in your body, closer to your true north, while respecting the busy body in you. Each direction—north, south, east and west—represents a different subject for reflection. In this meditation you will take a turn facing each direction while focusing on allowing everything surrounding that direction's topic to rise fluidly to the surface. Acknowledge all that comes up. Then ask Mama Ninja, the big earth spirit, Buddha, Allah or whatever highest source you jell with, to guide you to your own inner strength, solutions and intuition.

FIND A COMFORTABLE PLACE TO sit cross-legged. Close your eyes and imagine either the sun showering your body or the purification of a warm stream of rain. Think of all the things that shower your life with abundance, everything you are grateful for; now face west.

WHILE SITTING IN THE WEST:
This is the place of the setting sun. Think of all the things you are letting go of in your life—all the people, situations and locations. Shifting. Changing. Resolving. Behaviors you are letting go within yourself, friendships that are altering, jobs

that are lost. Allow it all to rise, ask for guidance and listen for intuition.

MOVE TO THE SOUTH:

This is the direction of grounding. Check in with how you are physically, mentally and emotionally. Are you drinking enough water? Feeling low on energy? Needing a little roll in the hay? This is the time to come home into your physical and emotional state. Identify where you are, and what you need less or more of.

MOVE TO THE EAST:

This is the way of the rising sun. Focus on anything new in your life: challenges, invitations, beginnings. Ask for grounding and guidance. Listen for your answers.

MOVE TO THE NORTH:

This is the direction of restoration and wisdom. Think of any wisdom or spiritual lessons you've learned or are learning. Think of recent wise advice.

MOVE TO THE EARTH:

Now touch your hands to the ground and think of the earth. Meditate on your "space." This could be the state of our earth, the state of your pad, the state of your friendships. Are there places that need cleaning? Attention? Love? Clarity?

WHEN YOU ARE FINISHED, TAKE a few deep breaths. If you are a list-lover then jot down specifics gained, or just trust that your soul knows and will guide you, inch by knowing inch.

CHAPTER SIX: TRAVELIN' LIGHT

"I've done it again," she said, head dipped low. "I thought I could quit on my own. I thought this was the last time. But I absolutely *couldn't* resist. They were Dorothy red, and it was two for one. Okay, the one pair alone cost more than rent, but then you get a whole pair . . . free! Can you front me a lil' cash . . . again?" When a loved one is caught up in a vicious shoe cycle, you alone cannot save her. Every time you solve her problem, you diminish her ability to solve it herself. Endlessly bailing her out, picking her up after a run, helping to find her car in the parking lot after a sample sale blackout, busting her out of Debtors Anonymous; all these acts do nothing more than circumvent her process of stumbling upon her own solution. It's like carrying luggage for someone every time they overpack—their muscles atrophy, their belief in their own ability to carry the weight lessens, while the resentment in your body grows.

THIS SACRED SKILL IS ABOUT flying right and traveling light, knowing the difference between helping and hindering. It's about developing the ability to identify what is your baggage and what is another's as dozens of pieces pass before you on the luggage carousel of life. The finest gift of flight you can give to your shoe-fiending friends (and to yourself) is belief and confidence in their own self-sufficiency.

Two ninjitsu guides to travel by: pack only what you can carry; carry only what you pack.

PACK ONLY WHAT YOU CAN CARRY

Don't expect a magic porter, partner or best friend to appear, ready to solve your problems, carry your share of the weight and eradicate all minor annoyances. Sometimes there is such closeness in a relationship that a half turn of your head, coupled with a .2-octave drop in vocal tone, translates into "something is horrifically wrong and you better hup-two figuring out just what it is or you *will be tortured*." It is healthier to actually endure the use of your vocal chords and speak up than it is to hint at your feelings and expect the other to read your mind and lift their bags accordingly. Intimacy among traveling partners? A good thing. The abuse of it? Not so good. Speaking your needs, solving your own issues? These are the vehicles to real spiritual flight.

ON AN INTERNET SURVEY THAT identified dominating person- ality characteristics, eighty-two percent of everyone I know voted my predominant quality was "Independent." And while I can navigate most anything, pretending to be fearless, I don't do so well when navigating involves words like "recon- figure," "network," and "USB ports." At my office the other day we were in the middle of a deadline when a torrential storm took the power out, shut down the network and made all of our work come to a dead stop. In my previous jobs I'd simply dial the tech department and go hide. But when you have your own business you *are* the tech department, you *are* HR, you *are* the after-work cleanup crew. All eyes turned to me, expecting that I might actually do something about our shutdown. Wide-eyed, I trekked through the rain to find the magic box called the circuit breaker. I reset the electricity, then renetworked our server. All cursing aside, I couldn't

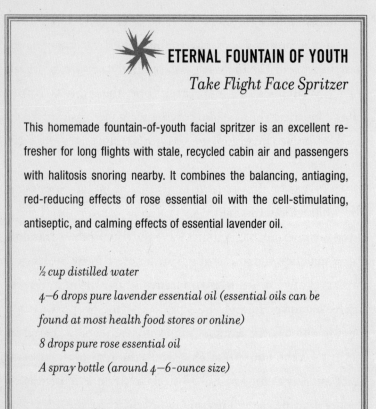

ETERNAL FOUNTAIN OF YOUTH
Take Flight Face Spritzer

This homemade fountain-of-youth facial spritzer is an excellent re-fresher for long flights with stale, recycled cabin air and passengers with halitosis snoring nearby. It combines the balancing, antiaging, red-reducing effects of rose essential oil with the cell-stimulating, antiseptic, and calming effects of essential lavender oil.

½ cup distilled water

4–6 drops pure lavender essential oil (essential oils can be found at most health food stores or online)

8 drops pure rose essential oil

A spray bottle (around 4–6-ounce size)

Combine and spritz away!

believe the effervescent feeling I had afterward. It was grati-
fication that just can't be matched by the relief of being saved
by someone else. When your power goes out, or tire goes flat,
or budget plunges like a skydiver down the Grand Canyon,
sleuth out the solution yourself. Don't go in assuming you
can't before you've even tried. Start making consistent ninja
assumptions that *you can.*

CARRY ONLY WHAT YOU PACK

If you are perpetually lost in the storms of other people's
problems, then (fancy that) you never have time to look down
the barrel of your own shotgun issues. It is a diversion tactic
all dressed up as "heroically helpful." Instead, why not devote
your time to delving deep into your own suitcase of spiritual
challenges, challenges waiting to be discovered, understood
and finally unpacked, and let others have the spacious grace
to work out their own puzzles. Less is more. Live light, travel
right, then take flight.

DOJO ON THE GO-GO
Travel Light

Anytime someone is fumbling with something, whether it's
finding a word, opening a jar or solving a big life problem,

practice using your ears alone. Offer suggestion only if asked, and even then say something to the effect of, "I support whatever choice you make, as I know it'll be the best one for you at this time."

For One Whole Week Practice Unpacking Some Bags

Practice reading through the entire instruction guide before asking for help. Practice getting your hands dirty fixing your own problems; solving computer, auto, work, what-to-wear issues on your own before enlisting experts. See how free it feels to lighten your load on your own.

CHAPTER SEVEN: IN THE RIVER

L ife is like a river—always moving, changing, gushing, rushing, whipping, brimming, frenetic, all at once— just like your Monday. You can either go with its flow or you can stand in the middle, waving your hands like a frenetic traffic conductor, and make futile attempts to stop it. I have acted like an obsessive-compulsive conductor at times, needing to control the exact longitudinal direction of the flow, at what speed it might run and toward which coordinate it will head, and then washing my hands in it repeatedly thereafter. I have tried to organize the river in a vain attempt to make others see my vision and promptly get on that plan. I've expected my assistant to handle phone calls for me per the script I wrote out with inflection marks and pauses noted. I used to expect that any given night would be just how I'd imagined it. I was always mapping, controlling. Exhausting!

Whenever I've tried to exert control over this massive river, I've always ended up getting flung around in its white-water rapids and spit out onto its bank, clear once again about who's the boss. The river. The impetus behind my tight tunnel vision is the deep-seated doubt that life, left to its own devices, will do me right. If I just control it "enough," then it'll be exactly as I need it, without deviations, disasters or random damages. Because there are no appointments held open for "chance brutalization" on my schedule.

Truth be told, I am not only resistant to arbitrary bruising like others of the human variety, I've been secretly resistant to *good* as well. Resistant to unexpected successes, windfalls or awards. The notion is peculiar, even to me. All I know is that I'm an extrovert of the painfully shy kind who acts like compliments are made of kryptonite.

What a stalled-out life; controlling the possibility of bad while rejecting the prospect of good!

Good, bad, or ugly, there really is only one choice—to be in the river and let her flow. It is in the river that miracles happen. If you are always controlling the exact nature of your route you will miss the brilliance of falling off the path and happening upon a field of posies that inspires you into a whole new chapter of your life. Stumbling down a dead end that brings you to your knees may teach you a new lesson that causes a total life awakening. But that only happens when you're open to the natural detours and undulations of life. When you have tunnel vision, with a rigid set of marks you want to hit in life, there is no room left for the river's plan for you. It is like being hell-bent on heading to an envisioned tributary. "Must get to tributary, must get to tributary. It has

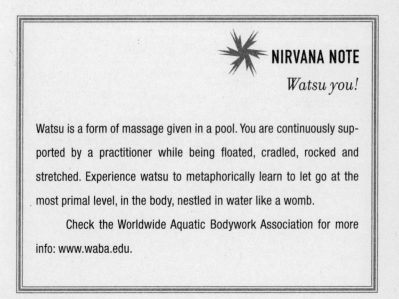

NIRVANA NOTE

Watsu you!

Watsu is a form of massage given in a pool. You are continuously supported by a practitioner while being floated, cradled, rocked and stretched. Experience watsu to metaphorically learn to let go at the most primal level, in the body, nestled in water like a womb.

Check the Worldwide Aquatic Bodywork Association for more info: www.waba.edu.

three whole kohaku koi, a picket fence and a trout I really dig." But the river. The river, man, the river wants to take you, sweep you up in her fury and brilliance, and drop you in her coolest, biggest tributary imaginable with gads of vibrant tropical fish, coral mistaken for jewels and a whole room full of dig-worthy trout. Get lost. Get swept. Go for flow.

The quest of the ninja isn't only to be in the river, but to *be the river*. Be the vigorous strength of the whipping current. Be the pliable fluidity of its changing waters—strong enough to withstand life's great waves of heartbreaks, disappointments and loss, but malleable enough to bend, not break, harmonizing with the ups and downs instead of bucking against them. The river is always morphing, moving, traveling, evolving, sometimes in silence and sometimes in a rage. Gorgeous. Big. Surging.

When you are in the river you know it; you feel it. It's the undeniable tickle in your nose, the calm in your gut, the inspiration climbing up your throat; the feeling that you are in your moment. Be in your river. Get tossed, get taken, get carried to your most limitless tributary possible.

DOJO ON THE GO-GO
The Rush of the River

This weekend, pick a day when you can spend five hours completely unplanned. Go in with little to no idea of how you will spend those five hours. Just let the current carry you. If you get an invitation, show up; if you run into someone, hang with them; if you feel an impulse to stop by the bookstore, stop and wander. Stay in the flow and let yourself relax without agenda, purpose or plans. See what comes up when you let it all down.

LESSON THREE:
DEFY

CONGRATS, NINJA! YOU'RE TEN POUNDS LIGHTER, DARLING, AND NEVER LOOKED BETTER! NOW THAT YOU'VE SHED ALL THAT ISN'T YOU AND YOU'RE READY TO SOAR, IT'S TIME FOR YOUR THIRD SACRED LESSON, *BELIEF IN THE SELF*. HERE YOU WILL LEARN THE ESSENCE OF ÉLAN, THE WARRIOR'S DEVIL-MAY-CARE SENSE OF CONFIDENCE.

CHAPTER EIGHT: THE LITTLE SHINKANSEN THAT COULD

When I was thirteen I was sent to the state swimming championship to race the butterfly. I was the only kid on the team who knew how to flap around like a spastic off meds and actually consistently propel myself forward. By the time my race was called, I was chock full of jumpy bugs from a dire need to pee. It had to wait; I didn't want to miss my race while in line for the loo. I was forced to sit through several heats until my number was called. I finally mounted the three-foot-tall launching pad, standing there as if on a ministage with everyone I have ever known surrounding me, including my new boyfriend, who already barely liked me more than Cute Stacy. High on top of that stand, bent at the waist, I waited like a petrified statue for the gun to say go, inviting me to enter the water and properly pollute the pool. No gunshot. But as I waited warm pee began to flood down my leg and I could not make it stop. Standing. Peeing. Standing. Standing. Peeing. Eternity. Painful. Everyone watching. Finally, *Bang!* I dove into the most smarting waters of my life, peeing and crying the entire several laps, trying my hardest to just keep spasming forward so I didn't come in last . . . twenty minutes after everyone else had dried off and run to the snack booth. What I realized while pissing, crying and spasming forward through said waters was that I *believed* in myself. I wholeheartedly believed, with every inch of me, that I never, ever wanted to be seen by another human being again.

Recently I revisited this great belief in myself on the night my roommate and I had our first ever housewarming party. I had spent a *good* amount of time making sure all of my outsides were fit, as I had invited every crush I've ever had to the party. The plan was that in one fair shot they could bear witness to how fetching I could be. Early in the night I went to "adjust the mood lighting," then quickly turned back to the party and went straight for the crème de la crush. Yet before I could even strut an inch forward I tumbled headlong over the ottoman into the exact . . . dead . . . center . . . of the party. Face-first. Now that . . . that was confidence. That was belief in myself. Belief that it could get no worse than falling face-first into the middle of your own soiree . . . and well before anyone was too drunk to care. I was bleeding with mortification. There was no option but to make like it never happened and scuttle off wide-eyed to the patio where a best friend poured rubbing alcohol down my bloody leg, just to remind me that a physical sting can be nearly as bad as an emotional one.

Moral of the story: one must spasm forth with *belief* in oneself. *Belief* that somewhere out there, there is a closet, with a lock and a swinging cat door through which three meals a day can be passed efficiently. And if you can't find your miracle closet, then you have to muster up a more sustaining sense of confidence. You must have assurance, not only to make it through life's urination mortifications, party traumas and other painfully earned social bruisings, but to really go after all that is on your wish list of life. As my gramma used to say, "Aim for the stars and make sure your guns are loaded." The thing about confidence is that you either have to be blindly, wildly self-assured regardless of the facts, or you need to be impeccably skilled . . . or you can "defy" all doubts and practice the belief of the ninja. A ninja takes her guns, the talents she already has, and then aims straight for the sky.

THE SHINKANSEN IS THE JAPANESE bullet train. To become a ninja you must take the Oath of the Shinkansen: vow to imagine this bullet blasting through all obstacles and fears to believe in the talents you have, like the little shinkansen that could. Could march into your boss's office detailing an ample list of reasons you have earned a raise; could apply for that international drawing competition; could speak your

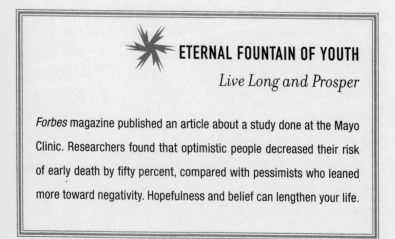

ETERNAL FOUNTAIN OF YOUTH

Live Long and Prosper

Forbes magazine published an article about a study done at the Mayo Clinic. Researchers found that optimistic people decreased their risk of early death by fifty percent, compared with pessimists who leaned more toward negativity. Hopefulness and belief can lengthen your life.

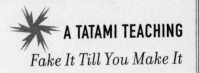

A TATAMI TEACHING
Fake It Till You Make It

When you simply can't believe in your shinkansen, fake it till you make it! Like a proper starlet, take on the role of a confident human. One method an actor practices to get into a role is to place the body in the character first. Physically putting on a particular pair of shoes the character might wear, for example, forces them to walk a certain way. Push the physical body to react differently, and the mind follows. If you wear shoes that force you to stumble around, you can't really walk tall and with confidence. This affects how others see you and react to you. Imagine someone really kickin', like Uma Thurman in *Kill Bill*, or Michelle Rodriguez in *Girlfight* or Hilary Swank in *Million Dollar Baby*. Physically see yourself as them, walk as if, carry yourself as if, and your mind will follow, believing what the body tells it: "I am confident, I am kick-ass, I am a walking aphrodisiac!"

mind to a group of men in a boardroom who resemble a crotch-grabbing fourth-quarter huddle; could tell that man for the first time, "Hell yes, I love you." All of the great warriors of the world share this in common—they have bullets roaring through their blood.

Take Joan of Arc, who was a mere peasant girl during a time when only men became soldiers. Think of the conviction this seventeen-year-old must have had to persuade leaders not only to let her fight, but to grant her a whole squad to lead. In the end this visionary was so on point that she had thousands of male soldiers lining up to fight under her. That took sheer shinkansen.

Take the great female samurai legend Tomoe Gozen, who fought alongside her husband. In one battle she defended an important bridge better than any male samurai. She was one of the only warriors left standing. She was known to charge straight into enemy lines, seek out the most renowned warrior and then behead him. Now that is one specific metaphor for your back pocket.

Take pioneer Annie Oakley, who began shooting game at the age of nine to feed her widowed mother and siblings. She developed the shinkansen to outshoot anyone, man or woman, earning the nickname "Little Miss Sure Shot." At *ninety feet* she could shoot a dime tossed in midair. Ya think that cat had her guns loaded?

IN COMPETITIONS, IN INTERVIEWS, IN life, in falling in love, you must believe in your bullets. Believe in your qualities and gifts. Own them. Honor them. Share them. Let the Oath of the Shinkansen course through your blood. It's time to defy.

DOJO ON THE GO-GO
Your Bullets

In "Breaking the Ties That Blind," you identified what your dream would be if you had no constraints. Now, list all of the talents and qualities that you have right now that will help you achieve this dream. Be generous.

CHAPTER NINE: WORDS OF THE WARRIOR

"I'm sorta thinking about maybe trying to become an iron chef someday, but I hear it's really difficult." As warriors we don't do *"maybe,"* we don't wait for *"someday,"* and we are never caught *"thinking about"*; we are caught in the act! Doing, being, manifesting . . . five minutes ago. In the last precept, "Fly," you weeded out all of the bonds keeping you blind. You developed your human bottom line, and cleared the path for what you really want out of this short, adorable life. Now it's time for sweet, hot action. It's time to defy! Yet how can you manifest something you can't even name? Speak, name, elocute exactly what it is you want . . . *as if it's already happening.*

An integral part of your warrior training is learning to pay specific attention to the words you use; they are more powerful than a satchel of samurai swords. Words are potent with power, they are the vehicles that deliver thought and initiate action. They are the skin giving form to a body. They represent how you think about yourself, the world and your place in it. When you continue to describe yourself in a particular way, it cements those ideas about who you are even further, leaving no room to evolve, change or emancipate from old narratives that no longer serve you, ninja chick. "I'm so bad with money!" "I am such a brownie whore." "I'm daffy when it comes to presenting in front of groups." You affirm the idea to others, who then reflect it back, cementing it even more, "Why don't I calculate the check, since you are horrible with money." "Hey, fudge fiend, leave a little for the rest of the office, Ms. Piggy!" "Don't let her present!" It also plunges you deeper into identification with the negative. As a ninja you will only use words of *katsu*, or victory! "I am enrolled in iron chef training and I will be a master iron chef, *hai*!"

Spiritual guide and sweat lodge leader Paul Eaglebear speaks about the power of thought and words before beginning any sweat lodge, an ancient tradition of purification

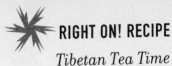

RIGHT ON! RECIPE
Tibetan Tea Time

Tibetan Buddhist monks living in the Himalayas drink a tea that they assert aids in digestion, promotes a healthy cardiovascular system, cleanses the body and rejuvenates inner strength. That's the good news.

The bad news? It's made with butter and salt.

Grab a friend and declare it "International Tibetan Tea Time." Take in the buttery yum while chatting about what you are actively doing to clobber your dreams whole. Chat about all that you are manifesting in your ninjitsu life using the powerful, progressive words of the warrior.

Recipe:

Water

Plain black tea

¼ teaspoon salt

2 tablespoons butter

½ cup milk or 1 teaspoon of milk powder

Steep tea, melt butter, add together, toss in the salt. "Enjoy."

where you state your intentions during several rounds of hellacious heat. He explains that when a word is spoken in a forest, scientists can decipher the word from the vibrations recorded in a nearby rock . . . the world receiving our sentiments. In the film *What the Bleep Do We Know*, pioneer scientist Dr. Masaru Emoto played with water crystals to prove the influence words have. Using high-speed photography and a powerful microscope in a very cold room, he took images of different water crystal patterns when various thoughts were directed toward them. The water exposed to loving words illuminated complex, beautiful, colorful snowflake patterns. When exposed to negative thoughts the crystals formed incomplete, disturbing patterns with dull colors. The earth?

✳ A TATAMI TEACHING

See and Say

Reflect back to others their highest self and that is who they will be for you. "You are so kind to me." Watch as they light up and strive to live up to that generous description even more.

---

seventy percent covered with water. Our bodies? Seventy percent water. The possible effects? Oceanic.

Shape your water's crystalline style. Speak about yourself with progressive katsu words. Don't wait for permission, validation or confirmation. "I am a sculptor." It doesn't matter if you haven't had a one-woman show yet; if you keep speaking with power, soon you will. People hear who you are, a sculptor, and introduce you to others as such, who then refer you to others with this thought in mind, and one of them happens to be a famous curator who wants to see your work on Friday. Actualization through intention verbalized. Henry Miller commented in a letter to Anaïs Nin that the support he had received was overwhelming, and that it seemed true social law that the more a person believes in themself, the more the world believes in them.

Now that you've cleaned up your mouth, clear out your ears. Listen for encouraging words and practice letting them in. I have been accused of being like a cup with a dozen holes; compliments are poured in, only to flow right back out. It is your responsibility to hear the compliments, take them in, fill your own holes. Hey, dirty bird, we are talking "cup" holes. If a person's words poured your way sound less "Rah! Rah! Kick 'em in the butt," and more like the cautionary, smoldering tone of the last cop who pulled you over, then get out of Dodge. In Lesson Five you will learn tactics on how to easily let wicked words roll right off your back. Take note if, every time you finally get up the courage to dive off into that grad program, you happen to tell *just* the person who barrels over your ambition with discouragement every time. Ask yourself: has it been easier to have my momentum reliably crushed and have someone else to blame than it is to actually go ahead and take the risk? Choose your comrades wisely. Always remember, the negativity of others has less to do with you than it has to do with their own fear projected onto you. Just see them as unrealized warriors and then slip them this book. ☺ As the Chinese proverb says, "Those who say it can't be done shouldn't interrupt those who are doing it."

DOJO ON THE GO-GO
Word Wise

Be extremely conscious of all adjectives you are tempted to use about yourself for an entire day. Be hypervigilant. If you are tempted to say something like, "I am so bad with money," work on altering it to, "I have been challenged with budgeting in the past, but I'm working on it and getting better all the time!"

NIRVANA NOTE
No Apologies Necessary

I read once that there is an overwhelming difference between how men and women respond when they bump into each other. The majority of women are quick to apologize, even if they were the ones bowled over by a runaway train with a BlackBerry.

One ninja friend commented, "When I used to work in a building with an elevator, I was amazed at how many women got on the elevator and said, 'Sorry.' Really, it's like one in three women do this, and no men ever do. I could never figure it out. Sorry for taking up space? Weird. Another woman, a brilliant young executive, preceded every single thing she said in business meetings with 'Sorry, but I thought . . .' "

Sorry diminishes the power of your opinions, all but writing off the point you are about to drive home. An apology is defined as: an acknowledgment expressing regret or asking pardon for a fault or offense. It is no grave offense to enter an elevator, take up space or have a point of view. Save your hearty sorrys for when you are caught half-naked with the new hot-hot-hot, barely legal mailroom boy in the Starbucks bathroom on your "sick day." Now, that's an appropriate time for a, "Goodness me, I'm just *so* sorry. There happened to be this spontaneous tornado alert and we hid in the bathroom and then there were aliens and chaos and a dog ate my clothes and cured me of my cold!"

Don't spend your life in one big apology; you are worth your warrior words. *You are a ninja, after all.*

Water Woman

Take five minutes today for some liquid meditation (we're not getting sauced by seven . . . at least not on this particular exercise).

Sit comfortably, close your eyes, take several deep breaths and focus on a clear, running stream. Imagine this stream coming toward you, refreshing you. Imagine in the water a stream of kind, vivacious words that describe you. If you are stumped, think of ways others have positively depicted you. Think of the water in your body, and the power of suggestion. The influence of these words shifting each of your cells, making you feel ten times better and look ten years younger!

CHAPTER TEN: KUNG FU FALLING

Accidentally peeing in public, falling face-first in the dead center of the party, completely losing your place in a pitch to a new client team because of your jack-hammer stuttering until you give up, fall silent, adopt a catatonic blank stare, turn and walk right out . . . episodes like these are evidence that you are in the game. After you've taken the Oath of the Shinkansen and feel the bullets of belief in your blood, the key to success is not in achieving flawless, fall-less, confident perfection, but in learning how to take chances and navigate the tumbles. It is called Kung Fu Falling, and a warrior is a master at it!

Traditionally, as boys grow up they are encouraged to

take risks, try new things, compete in sports, skateboard all night and bleed all over their Dickies. They become well versed in taking tumbles. Girls, on the other hand, are encouraged to value fitting into the group, never standing out and cooperating even if it means diminishing ourselves a little—or even a lot. Never the break dancing superstar, just

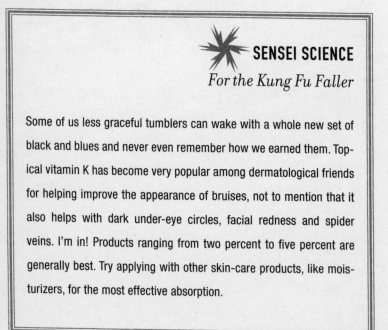

SENSEI SCIENCE
For the Kung Fu Faller

Some of us less graceful tumblers can wake with a whole new set of black and blues and never even remember how we earned them. Topical vitamin K has become very popular among dermatological friends for helping improve the appearance of bruises, not to mention that it also helps with dark under-eye circles, facial redness and spider veins. I'm in! Products ranging from two percent to five percent are generally best. Try applying with other skin-care products, like moisturizers, for the most effective absorption.

the girl standing by with the boom box. This has created a great reticence in many of us, a discomfort with falling, failing or even trying. Only one in ten girls will volunteer to try a new technology in the classroom, whereas nine in ten boys volunteer.

Ninety percent of having the confidence to try something new is rooted in your comfort with falling, even if it's in front of an audience suppressing laughter at your expense. Sometimes, when I used to surf, the ocean would give me a nice public humbling in front of a lineup of adorables. I would get knocked off the board, washing-machined to the bottom of the sea and rise completely disheveled with snot running out my nose. Despite having my ego shoveled down my throat, along with a pound of salt and sand, actually experiencing the fall and surviving it has lessened my fear of how horrible it might be. Sometimes I even manage to rise in a fit of laughter at my dorkitude because falling is freeing.

Bruises are beautiful, courageous to acquire and sassy to show off later. They are like postcards of ninja living.

Isn't it cool that when someone really sheds her ego and gets real, gets human and makes mistakes, it actually invites other humans to connect with her? When someone says, "I know it all; I've got it all covered," there isn't any room for anyone else to participate, relate or share wisdom. But when you are humbly fallible, you become more accessible. The anxiety of perfectionism lifts while fluidity and community step in. The biggest comfort is in knowing that your genuine loved ones stick with you whether you win a few rounds or fall in the first. So dive in. Try. Kung Fu Fall, laugh, get up. Stay up.

DOJO ON THE GO-GO
Kung Fu Fall

This may be one of the few moments in your career as a ninja when you will be told to fail, fall and feel free to make as *many* mistakes as possible. It is in the falling that the richest lessons are learned. When I'm too busy basking in the glory of winning a drag race I'm not forced to learn anything. But when my engine has broken down for the second time and I'm still paying off the first one, and the realization that it's my fault dawns on me, I learn a lot, *quickly*.

- Make a list of all of the times in the past, or right in the now, that you've resisted trying something new or really committing yourself out of fear of failure.

- List five things that you'd like to try in the next three months, under the direction that it is absolutely gorgeous to fall! Ninjas who fall and get back up are ninjas who become unstoppable!

CHAPTER ELEVEN: KILLER KOMPLIMENTARY KARMA

*I*n yoga the other day I couldn't stop compulsively stealing quick glances at Jen. Jen, whose very existence screamed, "Yes, in fact I was spat out with this taut, tan, perfect, glowing skin," was clearly adorable, obviously twenty-two and was my hot instructor's hot girlfriend who traveled the world by his raw-food-eating side. She rocked every move without cracking a tear or a sweat, had a body God made on her best day and had an incredible singing voice, which she demonstrated before every class by his side. Oh, and she just happened to be from *Brazil*. In a word? Jealous. Instead of being in my normal state of sweating uncontrollably while in a torturous rising sun sign of sadomasochism, I was additionally tormented by an obsessive comparison game (which, by the way, I kept losing).

Choosing to watch the surface of other people's lives is like watching promo videos—only the good times are on view, a nice stream of happy days set to an award-winning sound track. You can't judge your insides against other people's edited outsides. In short, it is very dangerous to go watching other people's promo videos. We have no idea how many takes it took to get that ten-second clip of bliss, or what happens when he goes home or what she struggles with in her head. If she's human, she probably spends some amount of time picking apart pieces of herself just like the rest of us.

Somewhere in my endorphin-induced yoga-high I realized that there *is* a choice, a way to deflate all of this power and assumption about "the other." Instead of "compare and contrast" or "compete," I can choose to "compliment." Revolutionary. I can jump away from "against," and toward an empowering "with," depositing ever more into my bank of good karma. Buddha knows, I can use all of the positive karma I can get, considering my wealth of debauched meanderings.

Like a simple kid with a pertinent question for the

teacher, I marched right over to Jen after class one day. I noticed a look of anxious hesitation as she saw me beelining toward her. I launched right in. "So check it out, you have a really beautiful singing voice," I blurted. All of the air in this overblown balloon seeped out and relief, admiration and a touch of nice breathed in as I felt her open and become slightly floored. After a few moments of silence she said,

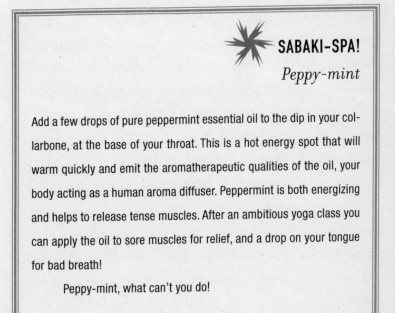

SABAKI-SPA!
Peppy-mint

Add a few drops of pure peppermint essential oil to the dip in your collarbone, at the base of your throat. This is a hot energy spot that will warm quickly and emit the aromatherapeutic qualities of the oil, your body acting as a human aroma diffuser. Peppermint is both energizing and helps to release tense muscles. After an ambitious yoga class you can apply the oil to sore muscles for relief, and a drop on your tongue for bad breath!

Peppy-mint, what can't you do!

NIRVANA NOTE

He's a Boob Man

Men love boobs. I know, a shock. Melons, peaches, ta-tas and in this case, "bust" love. Once I had an evolved boyfriend who discovered me nose deep in a *Bust* magazine. *Bust* is a progressive magazine "for women who have something to get off their chest." He started asking questions, took to my instruction, and promptly bought subscriptions for his sister, mother, and grandmother. He was a bust-loving, woman-loving man.

Many boob men apply for the job as our healthy samurai side-kicks and help to heal our world with us. They are the dudes beside us at breast cancer walks, the guys who recommend us for promotions, believe in our projects and stand up for us with words, actions and lots of knocker love. Cheers to boob men everywhere. You know who you are, and we luv ya!

"You don't know how much I needed that today." Later I found out through the yogic chai-vine just how much she needed it. Her sister had recently passed away and she could stand the little extra nuzzle.

One time I went out with this new guy to his friend's cocktail party, where everyone seemed just plain smart—smart lives with smart clothes and smart talk. The minute we arrived my date hightailed it over to some stunning female, lifted her high into the air in a "friendly" embrace and then fell away into smart conversation. He left me standing there like an a-hole in a near panic, feeling less than smart, self-consciously tugging at my "purse," an Astro Boy 3-D robot bag with a rock sticker partially tearing off. A few minutes later one fantastic ninja took pity on me and joined me for some comforting small talk. That guy was shortly dispatched to Category Friend. The woman ended up becoming one of my favorite confidantes.

Pivotal to ninja living is embracing the "code of the ninja": the discipline of remembering that you never act alone. You are a part of a fierce and damn fine tribe, a tribe that looks out for each other, and protects, guides, promotes, gives and receives together. Think of how *powerful* we are when we're on the same team. This is precisely the reason why whole eras of history abounding with suppression have skated by us. Women were burned at the stake out of fear of our incredible collective power. In all fairness, we've also lit the match a few times ourselves by creating divisions, thinking about resources as limited and being ready to claw at one another in competition. This happened in the eighties, like an experimental glitch. After ninjas worked so hard for generations to elbow our way into places like the ER or the boardroom, the first wave of working women morphed into man clones to survive on the all-male playground. I don't blame us; it was our best solution at the time. We took on masculine attitudes of exclusion and competition, and even tried to look like linebacking men with our shoulder-pad inserts. The pendulum is now flying back to the sacred feminine, the warrior power, and it's the ninja chicks who are at the forefront, believing in abundance, inclusion, the sharing of resources and bad-ass encouragement. It is the ninjas complimenting one another on bad days; it is the ninjas standing by each other, taking our side through uncomfortable moments, congratulating each other on big wins—more begetting more, support through thick and through thin. Lead the way, ninja chick, your comrades depend on you.

DOJO ON THE GO-GO
Super Sage Seven

Compliment seven women, one each day this week:

- two who you adore (this should be easy)
- three who intimidate you (this might be queasy)
- two who are perfect strangers (and this might be a bit cheesy)

Notice how you feel after each compliment. Notice the shift in your connection to "the other" when you take that first brave stride to reach out. Notice the revolution that occurs when you compliment someone who intimidates you. Most likely what you will find is that they have also been intimidated by you. It takes one to know one, and it takes one powerful ninja to recognize another!

Covert Mission

Seek out any ninja chick you don't know who is rocking in her job. Anonymously make a point to call her boss and tout her skills, secretly laying the way to her next promotion. Can you imagine what it would feel like to find out that some ninja you don't even know is anonymously rooting for you 100%?

Bodhisattva in Acceptance

Accept all compliments tossed your way this week. Simply thank the person rather than deflecting, denying or deterring the compliment. For the graduate ninja degree, write all of the compliments you receive in a month down in your ninja planner or Jedi journal. When I'm receiving feedback from a boss, all I hear is the criticism. She can make five great comments and one challenging one, and suddenly I have an overwhelming case of amnesia for the five while I vehemently cling to the one. Write down each compliment to refer back to when amnesia sets in.

CHAPTER TWELVE: LEAN INTO THE PUNCH

*I*f a fist flies straight for your face, what is your first instinct? To duck for dear life? Protect, hide and pull away, far from the punch? In the warrior's ring, if you pull your body away from the propelling power of a punch you are actually moving *deeper* into its trajectory, *giving it more time to land well*. A warrior in the ring learns to abolish all instinct to pull away from the punch. Instead, she pushes her body straight into it. It is only when you lean into your greatest fear that you inch just out of its path, actually too close for impact. This is the way of the ninja: to lean into precisely that which scares us the most, to head straight for the glove. It is in the heart of that white heat where the lessons are their hottest.

Fear is like a chunky, hairy, unshowered samurai with the sharp edge of his sword blocking your path, preventing you from stepping another inch forward. Denying fear only feeds it more power, rather than giving it a simple "Hey, how the hell are ya? Can I take your coat and your sword?" It's like trying to ignore an ex-boyfriend at a cocktail party. How

---

✳ **A TATAMI TEACHING**

Give the Slip

Ever heard of some kid who started a billion-dollar business because she simply didn't know any better? Her young ears hadn't yet heard all the "nos," "better nots," "it's too difficults" and "others have already done its." Sometimes ignorance is bliss. When going for your dreams, use the fighter's technique called "the slip" to slide right past obstacles. In slipping one rotates the body slightly so that an incoming punch passes harmlessly by one's head. As blocks, obstacles and opinions are thrown your way, sharply rotate sideways and allow those punches to "slip" right on by. Hear no obstacles, see no obstacles, receive no obstacles.

much energy does it take to summon up terribly attractive randoms to flirt with in front of him, orchestrating fake laughs for every moment when he might just glance over, while simultaneously avoiding eye contact and sneaking in obsessive peeks to see who he's with? How much easier is it to be the big girl, retaining every ounce of your power and confidence by immediately acknowledging him with your head held high, and then moving on to the rest of your expansive life?

Fear is like the ex in the corner; the more we try to ignore it, stifle it or stuff it away, the more space it gobbles up in the room. A ninja goes straight to the corner, straight to the core of her fear. One way to do this is to ask yourself, "What is the worst that can happen?" "If I do go up to him I might bumble, seem silly and look like I haven't moved on. . . . Okay so he thinks I haven't moved on and have a speech impediment. So then what? I'm thought less of by someone I don't even want to think about anymore?" Metabolizing the absolute worst that can happen is a cathartic way to relinquish fear. Tilt into the fear instead of dipping quietly between the ropes . . . straight out of the ring. It is only as you continually face all the fists, head straight for all the dark corners of your fear, that the power in them dissolves and you can lay your head down at night knowing no one and nothing owns you. Lean in and believe. Embody trust and then live as if no hit could ever keep you down, and none will.

DOJO ON THE GO-GO
Lean In

List the one thing you want to do before the end of your life, some kind of goal or even some kind of bridging of a gap in a friendship that you haven't dealt with in the last ten years. Answer the following:

1. What is the worst that can happen?
2. Can you accept that?
3. Imagine the best that can happen. Do a short visualization on how you would walk through it, face your fear and have the best outcome occur.
4. Now, let go of each of these results and, by the end of this week, take one first step toward leaning into that fist.

LESSON FOUR: EXPAND

YOU'VE GOT LOVE, LIGHT AND POWERFUL BULLETS AIMED HIGH. NOW IS THE TIME FOR EXTREME EXPANSION, NINJA. THIS IS THE LESSON ABOUT ACTION, ABOUT TAKING ALL YOU'VE LEARNED THUS FAR AND PRACTICING SOME VIVACIOUS APPLICATION. IT'S TIME TO EXPAND!

CHAPTER THIRTEEN: EXPANSIONS OF THE NUDE KIND

*I*once went on a hot springs retreat in northern California for a friend's wedding shower. On the way there one of the women mentioned that the last time they were at this particular resort there were "potentials" on the premises— i.e. good-looking men. I commented, "Yarks, brought the wrong bikini, shoulda packed the cute one!" Five women turned to me with curious stares. "Sweetie, no need for that, it's a *nude* hot springs," she explained. I pretended to be very cool. "*Nude*, huh, like nude. Like, not even underwear, nude? So then, I'm down with that, ya know, I do it all the time." Totally alone, in the comfort of my own home.

Later, as I peeled off layers, I made wild eyes at anyone nearby to ensure that no one would get any funny ideas and dare glance my way. There I was, sitting around buck naked with a bunch of strangers on a wooden deck. God love hippies. After the initial inconvenience of awkwardly trying to strate-

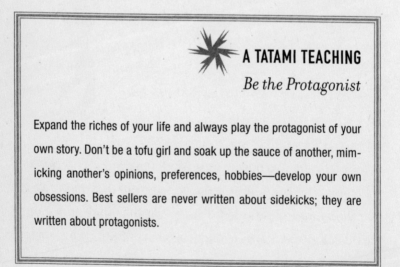

A TATAMI TEACHING

Be the Protagonist

Expand the riches of your life and always play the protagonist of your own story. Don't be a tofu girl and soak up the sauce of another, mimicking another's opinions, preferences, hobbies—develop your own obsessions. Best sellers are never written about sidekicks; they are written about protagonists.

gize the placement of extra limbs to cover privates, and the occasional accidental glimpse of a saggin' sack of boy-beans nearby, I found myself nicely "expanded." I was actually comfortable with something I never would have dreamed of doing before. In fact, halfway through the retreat I became the ambassador for "clothing optional," taking stark, raving nudity beyond the pool deck . . . down to the nature hike . . . around the campsite . . . through the communal market . . . because searching for the right tahini is always better cotton-free. I had never felt so liberated! Though I was not entirely sure everyone else at the retreat appreciated my newfound glory as much as I did. Had I not been surprised with the unexpected disrobing I never would have had this peculiar opportunity to learn how to be so comfortable walking around in my skin. Life as a ninja is all about dismantling, disarming and expanding. It is about taking the intuition you've honed and the confidence you've toned, all the work you've done, and diving straight into your hot springs pool of life.

In Eastern warrior culture the experience of life is called "life-death." There is an acknowledgment that each day you are living, your body is also dying. Pass the whiskey, it's about to get somber! Each day you are nearing your own mysterious "best-by" date, and as you tumble toward it you have a choice—to expand or to retract. Exercise your memory and stimulate all parts of your brain every day so there is no chance for atrophy. If you don't use it, you lose it! Use your muscles! Use your toes! Use your nose! Use your *soul*! Push the city limits of your spirit—your capacity for intimacy, the range of your experiences in life, your willingness to work through yet another argument with your friend, boyfriend, sister—because you might just learn something big, something that will birth you into a whole new way of being. Always practice. Always expand. Think of it as a circle drawn in the sand around you, an imaginary circumference. "I'm comfortable only going to these pubs, comfortable with this job, hobby, group of friends." If you push your comfort zone, push the perimeter a few feet farther out, your knowledge of the

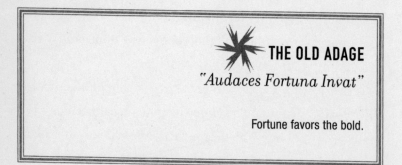

THE OLD ADAGE

"Audaces Fortuna Invat"

Fortune favors the bold.

world will become much bigger. Your knowledge of yourself will become leagues deeper.

The way to endless circle widening is with the declaration "Yes!" "Yes," the pet word of the precept. "Yes, I'll try the squid eggs. Yes, I'll come to your audience-participation performance. Yes, I'll go on a date with you, even though you don't even closely resemble my type. Yes, I'd love to try the

---

✳ RIGHT ON! RECIPE
Do the Cucaracha!

Use a shot glass and fill with the portions below. Light the drink on fire. It helps if you move the lighter in a circular pattern around the top of the drink and chant, "Fire, fire, fire!" Grab your cojones and shoot the drink through a straw. Be careful!

¾ of the shot is vodka

¼ of the shot is Kahlua

3 parts cojones

flaming cucaracha cocktail. Yes, please do teach me the Kama Sutra vadavaka pose. Yes, I'd love to be your new nudist cult leader." Stretch your willingness, push your comfort circumference and get naked to all the endless, incredible possibilities in your life.

DOJO ON THE GO-GO
Circle of Comfort

Draw a circle. In the circle make a pie chart of all the things that make up your pie of life (career, friends, family, health, happy hour . . .). For each piece of pie list five ways that slice of your life can be expanded, deepened and developed. After you make your lists, pick one area of your life and practice the five ways you can expand in that area this week.

CHAPTER FOURTEEN: FIVE ALIVE

5 4 3 2 1

*E*very once in a while I arrive at some appointment with a tremendously sweetened coffee in one hand, purse in the other and no recollection of how I got there, who drove me or how in god's name I was allowed to leave the house in such an unfortunate outfit. It's called "going auto," and it's a dangerous way to fly. Like a pilot who sets the plane on auto for a quick snooze, I space out while numbly moving through my high-speed daily list of to do. I am not there. Life is passing right before my eyes and I am on Pluto. You notice that this never happens with babies or lil' kids; everything to them is constantly new, carbonated, surprising, igniting. Miracles live in life's little details. Beauty lives

in the details. Burgundy and smiles and sweet scents live in
the details. After continuous bombardment of stimulus and
sheer repetition our senses numb to these finer points. Combat this by treating every experience, every moment, with a

✳ **SABAKI-SPA!**

Scrub a Dub Dub, One Fresh Bird in the Tub

This homemade rose sugar scrub is easy to make, antiaging and
leaves your skin with a dewy young glow. It's like a microdermabrasion for the body. It removes dead skin, helps with circulation (which
brings fresh oxygen to cells) and leaves the skin so soft and subtly
scented with petals from a rose. That's three senses down in one
scrub!

Jar (any ol' jelly jar, recycled bottle . . .)
½ cup of oil (use olive oil, or any oil for skin like almond or jojoba, found at health food stores)
½ cup of sugar (the smaller the granule, the softer the scrub)
Add drops of rose essential oil to your olfactory liking

blank slate, a newborn brain. A part of your ninja training is to commit to stay this conscious. Saturate the way you experience your day-to-day. Heighten and expand each of your five senses.

I was told a story by a Zen Buddhist about a meditation experiment performed on transcendental meditators (TMers), Zen Buddhists (Zeners) and regular people. In TM, a girl can really sink away deep into her meditation, whereas the point of Zen is to stay eternally awake, incredibly present and alive to every moment. In the experiment the TMers and Zeners were told to meditate, and the control group was told to sit comfortably and breathe deeply. In each group a loud, alarming noise sounded. The TMers didn't even register the noise. The control group registered it sharply and then stayed alert for some time. The Zeners registered it, then went immediately back to an intensely calm, meditative state. Next, the experimenters applied the noise with regularity. The TM group still registered nothing. The control group began to tune it out. The Zen group kept registering it every time as if it was the first—with a sharp drop, and then back to a meditative state.

This is the newborn-baby ideal and the goal of the ninja: to keep the senses completely alive to the world. Thomas Edison tested new research assistants by having them over for soup. If the candidate seasoned the soup before tasting it, he wouldn't hire them. He didn't want someone who made assumptions based on the past, habit or repetition. Treat every soup, every sound, every experience with five fresh senses. Expand your knowledge of the world. Receive her gifts, generously given in the nacreous hues of the insides of an oyster, the scent of cheap grocery store caramel-flavored coffee that brings you immediately back to the love of your grandma, the nearly inaudible soft, tumbling sounds of lofty snowflakes blanketing a silent street at night. By keeping your five alive, living is like one incredible acid trip without the whole, bad psychedelic tie-dye imperative.

DOJO ON THE GO-GO
Sensory Expansion
SOUND
Upon awakening, take one extra minute to listen to the world around you. Listen to all of the layers, near and distant. Then, all week, make a point to listen to music that is the extreme opposite of your usual playlist. Expose your ears to brand-new musical notes by taste testing internet radio stations

from around the world: Japanese Anime music, Uzbek pop, Mandarin radio, East African Vybezz, Swedish trance music!

SIGHT

Notice one color each day of the week. For example, on Monday focus on all the hues of blue throughout your day. This specificity pushes you to see past the blur of life speeding by and notice the finer points that make each shade unique—the cobalts, the indigos, the turquoises.

SMELL

Certain scents affect a person's mood. The smell of citrus brightens the spirits, lavender calms, vanilla seduces. Pick a scent to focus on each day this week and surround yourself with it at work, in the bath, in the kitchen, schmeared lightly onto your pillow at night. Rosemary stems, mint, fragrant tuberose, lavender essential oil, a bowl of oranges, a vanilla candle.

TASTE

Don't presalt your soup! If you are like me, then there are certain places you go where you never need to look at the menu. You order the same tuna melt with a side of balsamic vinegar *every time*. Expand your sense of taste all week by trying something new off every menu, every meal. Try the Korean yogurt soju, the menudo, the borscht, the turmeric masala; anything that expands your normal sense of taste.

TOUCH

Ah, touch. The easiest sense to dismiss in a world of constant sight, sound and taste. Touch. Reconnect with it. Each day this week spend one dorky, long slice of time closing your eyes and touching a new texture. The face of a loved one . . . does love have a texture? Memorize that face with your fingers. You can also do this with yourself. You know yourself two-dimensionally via the mirror . . . how about knowing your body through touch? Practice accepting and loving each inch you come across. Touch the earth, her damp, crunchy soil; the hairy leaves of a Dusty Miller perennial plant; the course texture of a brick; the soft waves of a stream of hair.

CHAPTER FIFTEEN:
"DO . . . AND WHEN NOT DO, BE"
(ANCIENT NINJA PROVERB)

"DO"

So far on your ninja rock-and-roll ride you've soaked your seeds with self-love, broken the ties that blinded and scribed your do-before-I-die list. You've seized the Oath of the Shinkansen, taken flight, learned to defy. Now you are *ripe* to fuse all of your lessons and go for the black belt of ninja living *and just "Do!"* Just dive in and do. Every tale has a beginning, every path a trail head, every marathon the first step, every tall tree the seeds and roots from which it first grew. Ninja, it's time to grow yours. My friend Paul Eaglebear once told me the tale of the oak tree when I came down with a bad case of the "no-ways" and refused to take any first steps. He said, "An oak tree must release her acorns, her gifts to the world. If she doesn't release and reproduce, she will perish and so will the forest. Holding onto your gifts does not benefit the woods. Go for your dreams without hesitation, let go of your best acorns; it is each of our responsibilities to the world. And when you do, remember that the oak tree cannot control how the seeds land or if they actually spawn new trees; just as you can not worry about how your acorns will be received or what might happen next. You can only be so courageous as to let them go." Which brings us to the next part of the proverb, "When not do, *be*."

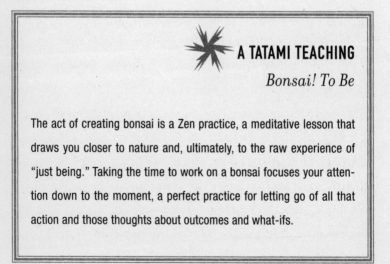

✳ A TATAMI TEACHING
Bonsai! To Be

The act of creating bonsai is a Zen practice, a meditative lesson that draws you closer to nature and, ultimately, to the raw experience of "just being." Taking the time to work on a bonsai focuses your attention down to the moment, a perfect practice for letting go of all that action and those thoughts about outcomes and what-ifs.

"BE"

After you've finished your series, sent in the application, made your follow-up calls, taken all the action you can, a moment of inaction is called for. It is the art of being. Weathering the hallway between yes and no. Simply letting go! It's like throwing a fishing line out to sea; you've taken the time to cast out your very best, given the line a hearty toss, and where it lands or what it catches is up to the undulations of the sea. Practice sitting still during those moments when you don't have all the answers. When the results do reel in, whether the fish is big, small or a bottom feeder, allow it to remain free from your sense of self. In the meantime, get drunk off of the gorgeous suspense. Now, just *Be*.

DOJO ON THE GO-GO
Starter Steps

In Chapter Four you made a list of what exactly you'd want to do in your life if you had no financial, training or time constraints. In Chapter Ten you listed five things you'd like to try in the next three months, under the direction that it is absolutely gorgeous to fall! Are there any congruencies in the lists? Take the strongest one and jot it down now. Now you are going to come up with three baby steps you can take right away to point your feet in the direction of that dream. Baby steps are manageable tasks that you can do in a day—like asking questions, finding out when a class starts, or asking around to see who has experience with it who might be a mentor or a guide. Want to finish that degree? Call information to get the phone number of the admissions office at the school you want to go to. After you've braved the first few steps, jot down what the next dozen will be and set a goal for when you want to knock them off. No matter what the results are, you will feel incredibly keen living in a state of action.

Ninja Loves the Lotus

A meditation to help you let go and just be.

- Breathe in slowly through your nose and twice as slowly out that same nose.
- Imagine your favorite flower at your heart.
- Imagine the color, scent and shape of each petal.
- Imagine this flower as your love center, quieting you down. Feel the sun warming it, the clarity of rain washing it clean of thoughts. Take as much time as you need, breathing deeply, really seeing this in your

chest. Visualize the bud slowly opening with a new strength and vibrancy.

- Now, buy yourself a dozen of those flowers today. If you can't afford it, there's always the neighbor's garden. But don't call me when your neighbors are telling you off while you're testing out your new trainers running the harjeezis out of there. That's not very sage of you.

LESSON FIVE:
CALM

AAH . . . ALL THAT ACTION, NINJA! YOU MUST BE EX-
HAUSTED. IT'S TIME TO COME DOWN FROM FLIGHT;
IT'S TIME TO LAND, TO LIVE IN YOUR SKIN, TO FEEL
THE ROOTS DEEP BENEATH YOUR INCREDIBLE
GROWTH. NOW TAKE THAT MOMENTUM, HARD WORK
AND ENERGY, AND MIX THEM WITH A CUP OF CHILL
TO BECOME FULLY INTEGRATED. THIS IS THE PRE-
CEPT THAT BALANCES ALL OTHERS. HERE YOU ARE
TRAINED ON HOW TO HANDLE CHALLENGES MAJOR
AND MINUTE, NEGOTIATE YOUR COLORFUL COMPUL-
SIONS AND DISCOVER THE POWER OF SEIJAKU.
WHEN YOU ARE THROUGH YOU WILL BE THE SVELTE,
SAGE NINJA WITH THE SWEET SMILE OF TOTAL CALM
ACROSS HER FACE.

CHAPTER SIXTEEN: TALE OF THE PISSING DOG: HOW TO HANDLE RANDOM A-HOLES, EPILEPTIC CITIZENS OF AMERICA BEHIND THE WHEEL, ASS GRABBERS, CAT CALLERS AND HUMAN STUPIDITY IN GENERAL

*O*nce I was walking up Fifth Avenue in New York City, past smart buildings with red carpets jutting out like tongues from entryways adorned by erect doormen. One doorman was escorting an older man from his car service to the front door. Also passing by was a happy-go-lucky-looking guy joyfully walking his happy, tail-wagging dog. He was the type of guy you pass and just feel a bit better for it.

His dog lifted his hind leg and released onto a tree all

that had been stored up from a night cooped up in a city apartment. The older man, whose body already seemed tight with anger, became irritated that nature took its course in front of his building and started ripping into the happy guy. I thought, "Wow, if my blissful day was interrupted by someone else's venom, I'd let the cat have it right back, thus allowing myself to get hooked into his frustration, joining him in cranky-town."

What the happy guy did struck me: he didn't seem to register . . . at all. It was as if he had headphones on, or was stoned off his sack. He just smiled, and not in that "I'm smiling just to piss you off, but secretly I'm fuming in a fiery hell of irritation" way. It was genuine. Like he understood, didn't agree, and wasn't going to join in the pissed-off party. He was just going to float right on by, totally unaffected. He embodied the best parts of happy dog living: forgetfulness, easy lovin', easy livin'.

Ever notice how a dog in a park will approach anyone with a smile and a ready tongue, even if the person still pinch-rolls his jeans, not caring whether he can afford a three-car garage or only a park bench? To a dog, it's just another human being, another opportunity to be petted, to experience touch, love and connection—or at least a hearty sniff. This man truly embodied the ethic of his pissing dog. "Just livin', man, just passing by, just enjoying it and ain't nothing gonna tear me from that feelin'."

"ACT THE PISSING DOG!" It's a hot skill set to navigate through this fishbowl we are all sardined in together. Choose levitation. Retain contentment regardless of the opinions or angst of others. I've come to realize that my happiness is my responsibility. No one can take it unless I'm willing to hand it

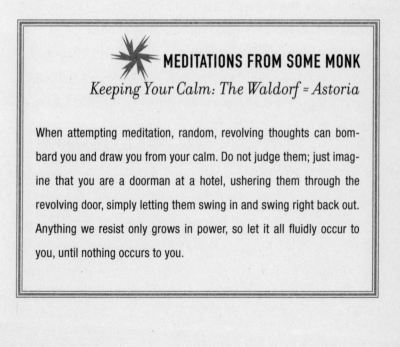

MEDITATIONS FROM SOME MONK

Keeping Your Calm: The Waldorf = Astoria

When attempting meditation, random, revolving thoughts can bombard you and draw you from your calm. Do not judge them; just imagine that you are a doorman at a hotel, ushering them through the revolving door, simply letting them swing in and swing right back out. Anything we resist only grows in power, so let it all fluidly occur to you, until nothing occurs to you.

over. Unfortunately, on some crabby days I am like TNT, more than ready for an explosion, waiting for someone nearby to strike a match and ignite my already short fuse. Then, with my mouth full of self-justified anger, I get to broil in my mood *and* have someone else to blame. Glory.

Pissing dogs and joyful owners everywhere realize that happiness is a choice. Pain is inevitable, but suffering? Optional. The first choice of the ninja is to *choose* calm; choose happiness, choose joy. The second? To guard it like a Hell's Angel. But how? How do you quell your wrath when a man whistles obscenities and makes those "fisk, fisk" sucking noises with his mouth while you are just crossing the street? How, when your coworker sideswipes you with, "You do always seem to gain weight in the fall, don't you now?" How do we navigate when random lemons plunge at us like a game of dodgeball?

First you must "get the lemon." Understand the nature of the citrus. That sour fruit spent a lifetime nurturing its tart taste on its tree of origin. Then suddenly you run into its branch and it falls on your head, knocking you out. You had nothing to do with its life, spent growing sour juices, or its ripe timing for a fall. You just happened to cross its path. Humans project chaotic family patterns learned as lil' fruits onto total strangers all the time, thirsty to heal these issues. It's an attempt at resolution, or simply habit to repeat what's become familiar. What people express about others within shooting range is very revealing of how they actually feel about themselves. For example, once a mistake I dated who happened to be very attentive to the details said, "Wow, I like the new, minute speck of gold eye shadow you started wearing," to which I snapped, "Don't look so closely!" thus revealing my fear that he'd use his keen sense of sight to pick me apart, not pick out the pieces he loved. Why would I presume that? Because I spend a darling amount of time picking my own self apart. It was safe to assume that others must be doing the same.

It always helps to know the origins of someone's lemons and limes. If you don't have the luxury of knowing the real source of someone's challenged attitude, imagine one. It's called compassionate imaginings. Do a little C.I. on the job. Imagine the person cutting you off like a crack fiend is actually rushing to the ER to see his mother moments before she bids adieu. Really. Try that one. Have you ever rushed off like that? I have, barreling 120 miles down to San Diego to see Gramma, my most favorite female running mate, just moments before she slid away. I drove like a crack fiend on the

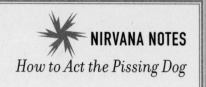

NIRVANA NOTES

How to Act the Pissing Dog

Note: Responses vary in degrees of compassion and sanity.

WHEN SOMEONE IS SPEWING NEGATIVITY AT THE OFFICE, DINNER PARTY, GROCERY LINE . . .

✳ Interrupt them and ask, "How are you? No really, how are you doing?" You might be surprised at the answer you get.

✳ Start spewing mundane, extremely detailed, boring stories until they are desperate to slip away: "And then when I was sixteen and in line at the DMV it vaguely reminded me of the time before, in 1982, when I was also in another line that was *just* like it. But I like lines, let me tell you about the line today . . ."

✳ Simply say, "I hope you have a better day," and walk away.

✳ Flash them the international sign of reason . . . two fingers of peace. And when in real doubt, the one finger of the bird.

✳ "Did Harrods have a sale on cruelty today? No really, I know you've got a kinder side. Invite her out to play, we do miss her today."

✳ This one particularly recommended for comments on your weight, bloating or general physical disposition: "You know, they say all of life's a mirror. Well, shoot, honey, I had no idea you felt that way about yourself. I think you look *just fine.*"

✳ Simply state, "Beauty is only skin deep, ugly's to the bone."

✳ Particularly good for strangers hell-bent on controlling everyone in a several-foot radius, bitching at you for not standing in line the way they'd prefer: "Sooo sorry, just got out of twenty years in the state pen, totally forgot all social rules of engagement, just been so darn long."

✳ Just smile for a mile; makes them wonder. Physically imagine their comment rolling off of you like water off the feathers of a duck.

WHISTLERS, GAWKERS, AND UNINVITED ASS GRABBERS

✳ Pervs often rely on a person's silence, discomfort and social training to make nice. Silence means consent, so combat this with voice. "Is that your hand on my ass, Mark? Do take it off." "Are those your eyes taking up rent on my breasts? I charge by the minute and right now, shoot, you're up to several bills. Maybe we should phone your wife and make sure you can afford it."

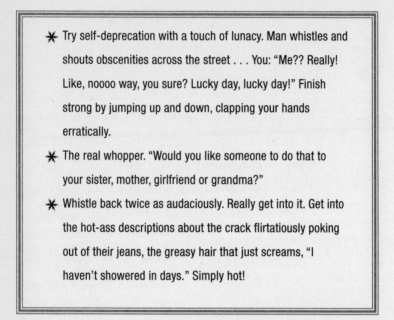

✳ Try self-deprecation with a touch of lunacy. Man whistles and shouts obscenities across the street . . . You: "Me?? Really! Like, noooo way, you sure? Lucky day, lucky day!" Finish strong by jumping up and down, clapping your hands erratically.

✳ The real whopper. "Would you like someone to do that to your sister, mother, girlfriend or grandma?"

✳ Whistle back twice as audaciously. Really get into it. Get into the hot-ass descriptions about the crack flirtatiously poking out of their jeans, the greasy hair that just screams, "I haven't showered in days." Simply hot!

dusty, emergency-vehicles-only side of the freeway, circumventing miles of stopped traffic, praying the whole way to Sampson, our family guardian angel, to protect me from retaliating drivers, honking horns and the highway patrol. I made it for a few last moments alone with Gram.

Compassionate responses are not just about kindness, ninjas, it is a matter of tactics. If we bite back it delivers on a silver platter justification for the other to say, "See, you *are* an asshole." It prevents them from ever having to look at their own behavior. It's like tennis—someone has to return the ball to keep up the game. Let the cranky ball drop and the match is over.

However, this does not mean making nice to every lemon-tossing twerp who rear-ends you. Compassion doesn't mean "lie down and prepare yourself for a good walking-on." On the contrary, it is founded on voicing the truth from a place of understanding. It's about sustaining your personal boundary and letting others know when their behavior is inappropriate. Enlightening someone in a calm way about their maladjusted behavior may be just the feedback they need to get real, and maybe even make lemonade. The point of this precept is to further the progress of mankind, no biggie. Own your sense of calm, and help others find theirs too. Inspire insight. Instigate communal heights. It's easy to meet bitter with bitter, spite with bite. Yet ninjas don't do easy; ninjas do impossible. And we look simply damn fine while we are at it.

DOJO ON THE GO-GO
Creative Imaginings

For one week concoct creative imaginings for any irritating lemonheads you run into. Imagine that the woman behind the SUV, with the cell-phone ear growth and poodle in her purse, ripping into the sweet old man who is searching madly for her valet ticket, just lost her loved one a day ago. Get creative. Go for compassion.

The Shit List

Make a list of a few people whose tongues tend to be sharp as a knife, jot down the times they've crossed the line and brainstorm centered, colorful responses that protect your calm, speak your truth and maybe even spread a touch of kindness. Yes, this is difficult; that's why it's keen to take a mo' to actually think it out instead of relying on your rapid-response system like a knee jerk that simply kicks them back in the balls. Although ball kicking can be satisfying, it doesn't particularly further peace on earth or make you a better ninja.

CHAPTER SEVENTEEN: STAYING CALM THROUGH HIRINGS, FIRINGS, BREAKUPS, BREAKDOWNS AND TWENTY-SIX-GAUGE NEEDLES

Now that you are a master in dodging randomly flung fruit, expert in dealing with the daily dishing of minor annoyances, how about the bigger episodes of life? What kind of calm does it take for the retching times, like when you became the solitary member of the Downloading Music for Free Society who *actually got caught*, subpoenaed and required to pay five thousand dollars, in full, in thirty days. Or the time when you discovered that your friend, who was kind enough to move your car into your new garage while you were away on holiday, somehow mistook 1242 Are You Kidding Me Street for 1270 What Are You Smoking Road, leaving your car for three weeks in some random person's garage. You come home to a tow notice with the friendly scribble, "You shouldn't go leaving your car in strange places." Noted. Cut to the tooth-impaired, laughing man behind bulletproof glass at the tow company spitting out, "Baby, it's only seven hundred dollars." What kind of calm does a good ninja employ for those darling days?

Situations like these are similar to being on an intercontinental flight with barf-teasing turbulence, mid-Atlantic. We are very much stuck for the ride, so we can either sit in

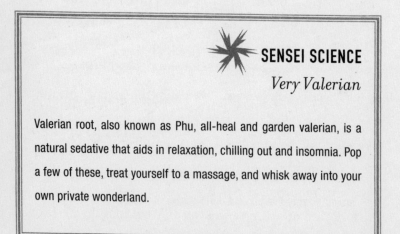

SENSEI SCIENCE
Very Valerian

Valerian root, also known as Phu, all-heal and garden valerian, is a natural sedative that aids in relaxation, chilling out and insomnia. Pop a few of these, treat yourself to a massage, and whisk away into your own private wonderland.

heart-palpitating anxiety, digging our nails into the arm of the passenger next to us at every dip and jolt, or we can realize that our panic attack won't help keep the bird in the air and utilize a little ninja calm. Although we can't choose what happens to us in life, we can always choose our reaction to the turbulence.

Rarely do we learn life's rich lessons while cruising at comfortable altitudes, so *invite the ride*. And for the times you'd much prefer *not* to invite the ride, invite a ninja sister instead. Like the time I went for the biopsy on my thyroid. I wasn't exactly excited about this trip, so I armed myself with a ninja sister, my best friend, Leapin' Lizard. Thank Buddha I did, since just before the biopsy they discovered that my darling nodule that was to be poked and prodded was completely

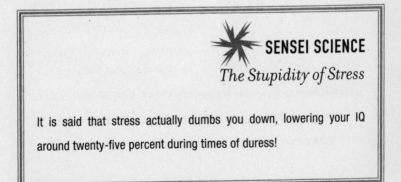

SENSEI SCIENCE
The Stupidity of Stress

It is said that stress actually dumbs you down, lowering your IQ around twenty-five percent during times of duress!

calcified. It was going to be extremely difficult to jab past the hardened calcification to draw out the sample cells they needed. After some debate the lunatics, or rather, radiologists, decided to give it a go, convincing me that the needle is normally only in for seven seconds. I can take anything for seven seconds, right?

The first needle full of anesthesia slid straight into the base of my throat, right at the subtle dip above my collarbone, a spot undeniably vulnerable. This needle *hurt*. They told me that the actual biopsy needle doesn't *really* hurt, but that most people are just frazzled by the odd discomfort and sheer terror. "In fact some have had to have their legs strapped down; one even had a heart attack." Really couth to tell me this moments before a needle the size of a ski pole is about to slip

---

Twenty-six-gauge Needle
Lesson Number One: Bring a Ninja.

We are a collective community; we never have to do anything alone. People live longer when among other sentient beings. Take advantage of this proximity and grab a friend for the ride.

---

into my skin. If I didn't have Lizard there, saying soothing words while I cut the circulation off for her entire right arm, I would have been heart attack number two. To be honest, I had actually begged her not to bother to attend the day's ceremonies. I knew it was her first day off in two weeks and I thought it wise that I play the part of James Dean for the day. Like a true ninja sis she didn't listen to a word I said and demanded to go.

Ouch! The biopsy needle plunged in. Deep. It felt as if it was digging for gold at the back of my throat. Seven seconds of the needle poking passed. One minute . . . passed. I stared at the ceiling in absolute terror, trying not to move a muscle and botch the entire team effort. Trying to remember, "Oh yes, I should be breathing. Breathing yes, moving no."

Twenty-six-gauge Needle
Lesson Number Two: Breathe.

Elementary, but not when in a panic. Deep breaths are known to slow the racing heart, infuse the body with oxygen-rich, calming blood and ease mental horror.

As a meditation, I pinpointed all my concentration on my breath . . . the needle was *still* in me. Focusing on the breath draws the attention away from the storm and into the calm. It's one of the simplest, most ancient, tried-and-true forms of meditation, available at a whim, always only one

---

Twenty-six-gauge Needle Lesson Number Three: Remember, You Are a Ninja, Part of a Sacred Tribe of Fierce Women

Sometimes you are asked to deal with the sharpest turbulence this ride can toss, and other times you have to field all of the minor bumps along the way. Like the time you just happened to stumble across the BlackBerry of the guy you were dating and you accidentally looked through every single e-mail, contact and text from the previous two months only to discover a note from someone that was not you. "Had a great time Sat. night, thinkin' of U, x o x o, smooch & smooch." Ode to life's undulations! React to them with the sanity, dignity and strength of the ninja that you are—that is, after you toss him, his newly broken BlackBerry and the baffled look on his face straight out your front door.

MEDITATIONS FROM SOME MONK

The Quickie

This meditation is your "just add oxygen" quickie to use at a moment's notice, like when that a-hole cut you off after tailgating you for ten miles; or when your coworker takes credit for the idea you've worked on for months; or when you run into *him* with a new her. This is the on the spot emergency meditation.

Stop all thought. Focus on your breath, breathing only through your nose.

Take a deep, slow inhalation, lasting at least ten seconds. Let out that breath even more slowly.

Concentrate on pushing and pulling the breath through the back of your throat, not just your nose, as if your throat is a wind tunnel. It's called an ugi breath, and can sound like Darth Vader.

Now, imagine that your face is made of warm clay that is heavily relaxing, falling gently to the sides. Move down to your neck. Relax the muscles, feel your shoulders release and fall back down away from your ears. Keep moving down your body, one muscle at a time, each like a loose weight of warm clay, slowly releasing.

Feel your feet touching the ground, and remember that mama earth is supporting you. Feel the roots of her connected through your feet, channeling strength up to you.

breath away. Finally, they were out. Aaaaaaa; my whole body sighed in relief from the sterile, stiff tension.

"We're having trouble. We've got to go back in, and it may not be the last time," they said. Oh my. I thought I was in for a sprint, not a freakin' marathon! I had to tap serious, primal, warrior calm. Because calm I was not! In they went. By this time tears silently streamed down my cheeks as I stared at the ceiling, thinking, "I am such a wuss. I am the queen of the wuss brigade. Wuss wuss wuss, wait. Stop! I command you to stop. Stop it, you wuss! I am . . . I am somewhat a ninja. I am a ninja and I am a part of a tribe. A part of a large crew of fierce ninja chicks who have survived this, and more, with strength and character." I repeated over and over, "I'm a ninja," tapping into some universal strength that triggered an anchoring layer of calm.

Get in touch with that primal sense within and tap your well of strength, the same strength that thousands of ninjas for hundreds of years have drawn upon through violent adversity and everyday challenges. Use names for yourself like Irrefutable, Strong, Healthy, Capable, Ferocious.

Practice these three ninjitsu keys to calm in all your adventures. First, bring another ninja, either physically or mentally, and spiritually "back pocket" a few while in interviews, emergency situations or tough times. Second, breathe. At a moment's notice you can ground your entire body, calm your soul and it's always only a breath away. (Try "The Quickie" breathing exercise for immediate emergencies.) Finally, don't ever forget your stock: you are a member of an esteemed society of rebellious, righteous women who *live* for the ride.

DOJO ON THE GO-GO
The Box o' Bad Day!

Ninja's night out; invite some friends over. Ask each person to bring a closed box of any sort with a slit at the top (shoe box, Gramma's old jewelry box). Put out recycled paper and colorful pens. While sipping on libations and ingesting solid amounts of sugar, write each other sweet, secret messages on paper and put them into each other's boxes. Write things you admire about the others, anything that would make them smile. This is now your "Box o' Bad Day," to be drawn upon during rough rides.

CHAPTER EIGHTEEN: CALM THROUGH UNCONTROLLABLE COMPULSIONS

Holidays are the perfect breeding ground for compulsions, like a petri dish filled with bad behavior multiplying by the millisecond. One New Year's Eve, for example, I had all of my *most favorite* humanoid defects on overdrive, as if to make my New Year's resolution list abundantly clear and, well, quite long. As we neared midnight I found myself compulsively causing arguments with the guy I was dating, at one point because he complimented me by saying, "You're the tallest woman I've ever dated." Instantly, I started thinking, "Oh, *rrrealllly* now." "So does *that* mean you normally date shorties? Petite girls? Right? You prefer them,

don't you?! You prefer anorexia, don't you?! Howdareyou-
Iknewit!"

PICK YOUR OWN PET COMPULSION: cocktail-fueled temper-
tantrum Tourette's, uncontrollable hoovering all of the holiday carbohydrates in sight, doing your part to contribute to
the national debt and the back pockets of credit card institu-
tions everywhere, smoking all night in an attempt to main-
line nicotine, stopping by your ex's accidentally every night
after last call (to name a few) . . . By the way, you sound like
my kind of ninja! When you are having a good bout of your
pet neurosis, what is the first thing you naturally want to do?
Dive headlong into that impulse, *now*, and fill 'er up, right?
But if you always turn to these outside sources to satiate momentary impulses, then you become reliant on them. You *always* need something outside of yourself to intercept any
feeling you might be having and *fix it*. Those external fixes
are, unfortunately, temporary. The hot Brit flies back across
the pond, the sugar crashes in twenty, and the new sweater
loses its dazzle the minute it moves from boutique to home
closet.

   During those special few times when I've sat through an
uncomfortable experience and reached for nothing beyond

my own seedling strength, I've expanded miraculously and felt all tickled inside. This is the ninja way, to draw on our inner resources through tumultuous, obsessive times. Owning this inner ability builds an incredible, edible power that is untouchable and totally delectable. It creates the space to experience something *bigger*. Something beyond the limitations of what you think you can handle. Something possibly even spiritual. Revolutionary. An experience that doesn't just momentarily carry you past the feeling, but lifts you into your highest kick-ass-ninja self, which pounces straight *through* the feelings, challenges and issues.

Now, that sounds cool on paper, but what about off the page? How do you really, truly use inside resources to calm

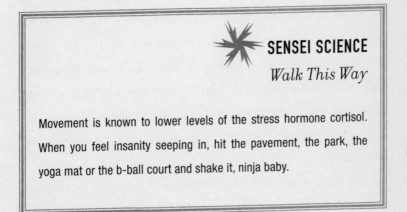

SENSEI SCIENCE
Walk This Way

Movement is known to lower levels of the stress hormone cortisol. When you feel insanity seeping in, hit the pavement, the park, the yoga mat or the b-ball court and shake it, ninja baby.

yourself through temptations for a cigarette after having quit for *twelve months*? How do you stop from throwing your face mouth-first into the last piece of cake that you had thrown away in the trash but took back out because wasting food is bad and maybe you just want another nibble? Personally, I need a foolproof warrior plan for my momentary bouts with madness.

Smoking-cessation studies show that cravings only last ten minutes, at the most. If you succumb to that craving, then the next urge arrives earlier. If you can resist, those intense ten minutes become more spaced out. It's about brain training. It's about outlasting those ten minutes, even if you have to do it two hundred times a day. You grow new habits by consistently practicing them, thus retraining every last synapse in your brain. As Einstein said, "The significant problems we face cannot be solved at the same level of thinking we were at when we created them." Below is a breakdown of what to do each minute of your own personal ten-minute moment. (Ma'am, put down the cookie. Put down the cookie and no one will get hurt.) If your impulse is to pick up a weapon of mass sedation as a calming solution, just give it these few minutes first. Set your clock, time yourself, and relentlessly commit to each step.

MINUTE 1: PICK A POSY AND JUST BREATHE

The first step is to create some space before instantaneously fulfilling your impulse, so you can have room to choose a new response. Promise yourself that you can have whatever it is you're about to dive off into, but you have to take this ten-minute pause first. For the first sixty seconds, take deep, continuous breaths. Grab something tactile, like a petal from a posy. Feel the flower. Be the flower. Zoom all your focus and thought for a moment on the petal—the silky touch, the vibrant color, the intricate vein patterns. Centering your focus will help you bring yourself back to where your feet happen to be standing, and away from the obsession of replaying what he said, she said, then I said, and maybe I should call back right this moment and say it all! Focus on where your feet are—in the moment!

The petal is a good visual reminder of the moment. Soon it will wilt and fade and disappear. Don't hold on too tight, or fear that things will never change. Let the feeling flow through you like sand passing through your palm. You can't clutch onto the sand. Just let it flow. Being in the moment connects us to our bodies, and when I'm about to dive into neurosis I often find that I'm not only out of my mind, I'm usually out of my body, too.

MINUTES 2–3: USE YOUR NOODLE

Think well past the moment and get colorfully descriptive about how you'll feel after the impulse is indulged. What will your tummy feel like? What will your day feel like after waking up next to your ex? Ouch. Think it through. Impulses, by nature, are instantaneous. They're typically satisfied because we don't take the time to think them through past the immediate enjoyment. So take the time to remember that just around the corner lurks the hangover, the withdrawal, the heavy emotions, the *regret*.

MINUTES 3–5: SEE THE NINJA

Focus on what you are gaining (strength, self-love, clarity, more time to pursue dreams . . .) and not what you are giving up (the cigarette, the false sense of momentary calm). If you think only of what you believe you are denying yourself, then the desire for that very thing will grow like the plant in *The Little Shop of Horrors*. Feed me, Morris. Feed me!

Focus on what you are gaining, and hold in your mind's eye the woman you want to be *as if you are already her*. Imagine you are the ninja who has already stopped incessantly biting on her cheek, or stopped her last-minute runs for a double-fudge fix. If we went crunchy for a moment, we'd say,

"Hold this image in your top chakra, where your third eye is, at the meeting of your eyebrows." Visualize the entire, empowered scene of you succeeding. See the ninja; see what you are gaining, becoming.

MINUTES 5–10: CHECK YOURSELF BEFORE YOU WRECK YOURSELF

Check in about why you want to check out. Usually, when I'm craving to check out, it's because the feelings that are sinking in feel too thick. Now it's time to delve deeper, to dig into what is causing the need to seek ease. Free write to unwind the thoughts bogging you down, or call a friend and unload. We're only asking for five minutes here, so put pen to paper, doll. Five minutes is worth the incredible changes that are about to erupt. If you hit upon an emotional geyser, don't stop at five, just write it out . . . right it out!

TEN-MINUTE STIPULATION: THIS ISN'T about being a "good little girl" and doing it all perfectly. This is about being a *ninja*. And ninjas never do it autobot-perfect. We do it in a raucously, beautifully human way. It's about having a full life, not a Clorox-clean one. This isn't about cutting out the fun; it's about recognizing the difference between need and enjoyment.

* * *

FUDGE-FACED ADDENDUM: WHEN YOU come face-to-face with the double fudge you may consciously and quickly toss the Ten-Minute Moment technique aside because

a) you know it may just work, and

b) you want what you want when you want it more than you are able to want what you want for yourself in the long term.

So if chocolate is already dripping from the corners of your mouth, you sweet-toothed ninja, don't beat yourself up. That merely keeps you closer to the cookie. Self-punishment breeds bad feelings, which thrust you back into the cycle. "Well, I've already ruined everything eating one, so I might as well eat the neighbor kids' entire year's supply of Girl Scout cookies." Stop where you are, put down the cookie, put down the blame and gently accept that you just evidenced your humanity. Now recommit to being the ninja you want to be. Gentleness breeds gentleness.

DOJO ON THE GO-GO
Pause for Your Pets

Your assignment is to be *über*conscious all week of the times when your pet compulsions come up. Is it whenever things heat up at work? Whenever you get insecure about a certain something? Take a pause and choose a proactive, positive new way to act, as opposed to any instant grabs at temporal comforts. Notice your first impulsive reactions, curb them, and practice conscious pro-action.

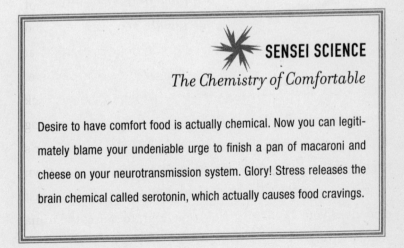

SENSEI SCIENCE
The Chemistry of Comfortable

Desire to have comfort food is actually chemical. Now you can legitimately blame your undeniable urge to finish a pan of macaroni and cheese on your neurotransmission system. Glory! Stress releases the brain chemical called serotonin, which actually causes food cravings.

Blue Ribbons and Rose Petals

Grab a ninja or two for this exercise. Get together and identify the compulsion you are working on letting go of. Just
pick one, you ambitious ninja. Set some goals for the week in
regards to the obsession. Now pick a posy, and at any point
in the week when you fall out of the moment and want to obsess on "Why in god's good name is my client taking over two
weeks to get back to me on this life-changing proposal!"
touch your petal. Then, at the end of the week when your goals
are met and you rock your ninja vision, give each other surprise blue ribbons! Put them on each other's car, front door,
office or refrigerator to congratulate, encourage and remind
everyone nearby how "colorful" you are.

CHAPTER NINETEEN: THE POWER OF SEIJAKU

*T*he other day while I was speeding in the fast lane, late to an appointment, I had an epiphany of the busy body kind. I was in midmultitasking mode: Clark Kenting my entire outfit behind the wheel, a half-peeled banana named breakfast on the dash. Phone? Clutched between my neck and shoulder. Hot coffee? To my right. Directions to where I'm going? Plunged in the black hole of used water bottles on the passenger floorboard that I call my "recycling project." As I sideswiped two lanes over—nearly plunging into a ditch because god knows I can't have coffee without a few packets of Splenda—the thought occurred to me, "I try to do too much at once." I'm addicted to adrenaline, addicted to fast, more, now, quick, hurry, loud, get it all done in a day, *über*productivity. I'd live off a vein-injected caffeine drip if I could. Silence is not something I do. It takes a miracle or a controlled substance for me to sit still. Still is for the more fortunate souls who spend high percentages of their time in downward dog, eating bowls of vegan quinoa.

Because I am so calm averse (with natural masochistic tendencies), I decided to do a home "silencing" and spend forty-eight hours without ingesting a single ounce of stimulus. No television—not even HBO—no books, phone, Internet, or talking to another human being. By 9:29 a.m. I *didn't*

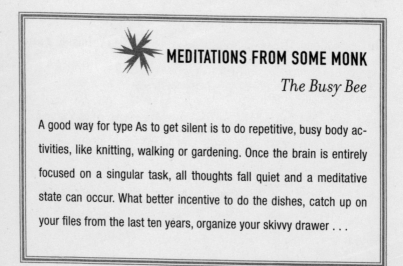

MEDITATIONS FROM SOME MONK

The Busy Bee

A good way for type As to get silent is to do repetitive, busy body activities, like knitting, walking or gardening. Once the brain is entirely focused on a singular task, all thoughts fall quiet and a meditative state can occur. What better incentive to do the dishes, catch up on your files from the last ten years, organize your skivvy drawer . . .

know what to do with myself. I quickly learned how habitual my reliance was on social noise. Arriving home, I instantly turned on the music, checked all five e-mail accounts and listened to voice mails from two different telephones. The forced period of stillness was refreshing, like clearing my cache or wiping clean my cluttered blackboard. Everything felt so enunciated afterward. I could hear new layers of sound, and feel every little nod from another. I was able to experience each nuance that I normally ignore in the face of the forty things I'm trying to accomplish all at once.

Seijaku, or using the power of silence, is an ancient warrior skill important to cultivate. It is in silence that you land, come home, refresh your mind and restore your senses. In this calmness, the mud spinning in your bucket has a chance

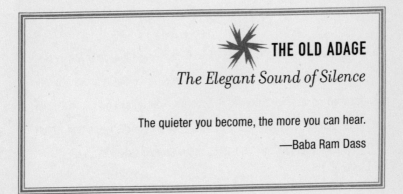

THE OLD ADAGE

The Elegant Sound of Silence

The quieter you become, the more you can hear.

—Baba Ram Dass

to settle. Only then can you see clear waters again. As a fully integrated ninja, you must learn to take all of your extreme expansion and fearless acts of flight in company with the soothing moments of taking some pause. It is when you are quiet enough that you can mindfully hear all that is intuitively screaming out to you. Silence is your teacher. Take some time alone with her daily and listen for what she has to say.

DOJO ON THE GO-GO
Tune In, Turn Off, Drop In

Do a twelve-hour day silencing. Take a day completely to yourself, turn everything off and tune on in. Get lost, get quiet, thrive in the silence, listen for what comes up. When you are done, write a paragraph of what you'd like to retain from your day of seijaku, to take back into your highly stimulated life.

LESSON SIX:
GIVE

YOU'VE REACHED THE MOST CRUCIAL PRECEPT, "GIVE." IN THIS FINAL TEACHING YOU ARE INCULCATED WITH THE LAST SECRET, THE MOST IMPORTANT GIFT YOU CAN GIVE TO THE WORLD. IT IS HERE THAT YOU LEARN HOW TO PASS THE PRECEPTS ALONG, FOR IT IS ONLY IN THE TEACHING THAT LESSONS TRULY CEMENT WITHIN THE SELF. IT IS ONLY IN THE RELEASING AND RELINQUISHING THAT WE ARE LIGHT ENOUGH TO RECEIVE AGAIN. THE TRUE MISSION OF A NINJA, THE SLY GIRL BEHIND THE SEXY MASK, IS TO SAVE THE WORLD, ONE MISSION AT A TIME, ONE GIFT AT A TIME.

CHAPTER TWENTY: THE MOST IMPORTANT GIFT TO GIVE

Quitting your job on Wall Street to go help starving babies in Somalia? Good work. Taking your morning to mentor a little sister and your afternoon to save the local deciduous tree forest? On your way to warriorhood with a splash of fourteen-karat karma, to be sure. But let me tell you a little story about a boss I used to have. This was a woman who was in the business of saving the world. She worked for nonprofits and nongovernmental agencies around the globe, and her work changed lives. So did her attitude, which was so tightly wound that anyone within striking distance was left lashed by her eruptive, unraveling coils. This was a woman who, five minutes after solemn meditation, could be found yelling holy heck at her scurrying puppies. What, really, is the karmic tally if a person tosses a little green in the corporate holiday charity basket, but then runs around acting like an institution-worthy raving lunatic to the entire office staff, leaving people scorched for life?

Being the best you is the purest gift you can give to the world, or at least it's an honest start. Speak kindly to yourself and to others. Act generously to yourself. Ditto to your brethren. Treat yourself with respect and others with meaning. The most human gift you can give to another is to simply acknowledge them. To take the gentle time to look right into his or her eyes, give a smile and connect. One time I was walking home and there was a homeless man camped out on the walkway, expressing himself "theatrically." Like a fighter

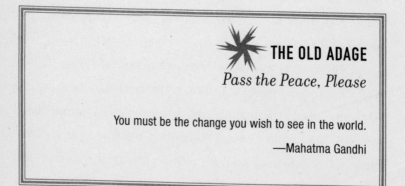

THE OLD ADAGE

Pass the Peace, Please

You must be the change you wish to see in the world.

—Mahatma Gandhi

fish circling, he was puffing out his fins, scaring everyone off from his territory. It seemed to me like he was acting the way people expected him to act. So instead of walking around and avoiding him, as he may have been used to, I walked in front of him, and as I passed I looked him right in the eyes for one supple moment. Then I saw something happen. He lowered his paper-bagged drink, softened his bravado, became human, looked me right back in the eyes and asked in a calm, gentle voice, "How are ya tonight?" I answered, then asked him how he was, to which he said, "I'm blessed. Thank you for asking." Often the gap between us is so great, and it's just fear. Challenge that space in between. Walk tall and look deep. Pause. See another. Allow yourself to be seen.

Last Mother's Day rolled around and, in a giftless panic, I concocted a lame poem and a promise to spend the day volunteering in my mom's name. It was the first year without my grandma, who had been one of my best girlfriends, so I decided, "If you can't be with the grandma you love, love the one you're with." I bought a bucket of gerbera daisies from the farmers' market and took it to a local elderly home that I picked out of a phone book. When I asked at the nurses' station if I could make rounds giving out the posies they just stared at me, perplexed, as if I had strolled in off the previous night's psychedelic trip. Regardless, they nodded yes and sent me off.

Nervously, I went to the first lady's room. I sat with gramma number one, flower in hand. I believe I was shaking from a sudden case of the total humbling that comes with the soft reality of life. Of aging. Of truth. "What is your name?" I stuttered to the woman, who had milky brown eyes, a tender, open face, and snow-white hair. "Well, hmmm. Well . . ." A long, fumbling pause as she searched desperately for her name, until I said, "That's okay. Half of the time I can't remember mine, either," every word choked off by a tear wanting to push itself into the party. At the door to her room a guy wheeled on over, wanting to know what the commotion was about, then another curious woman rolled in, and soon I was surrounded by a wheelchair gang, questions flying all the way around. One woman asked what I did for work. When I mentioned my jewelry business, she asked if I had made my necklace, to which I uncomfortably replied, "Yes." I was a bit shy to show her the skull and crossbones pendant that exclaimed, *Bad to the Bone.* She leaned in and exclaimed, "Oh, it's *just* beautiful!" That pushed me over the edge and to the moon. It was too sweet. Too real. Too elating and grounding.

Just listening, letting someone exist; that's the gift. I showed up to be the ear, but then I was touched by feeling heard. Allowed. Accepted. Received. That day listening, giving, receiving, did not bring a close to any worldwide wars—didn't even feed the hungry—but it fed a bit of the hunger in my soul for life. It brought a bit of the kind of solidifying peace inside that emanates out, healing by ounces and inches and, hopefully, humbly adding to the communal healing our sweet world is thirsty for.

This imperfect planet needs a ninja more than ever. Needs your peace, your most whole, pure self. As a warrior on this honorable path, you are being asked to call up your highest self and then give your best you to this little planet called home and to all of its erratic, imperfect inhabitants.

DOJO ON THE GO-GO
Windows to the Soul

For one day, concentrate on looking into the eyes of everyone you come across. Notice what challenges come up; notice the simple elation of connection.

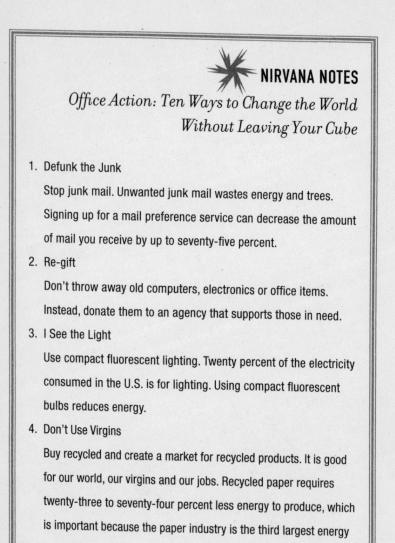

NIRVANA NOTES

Office Action: Ten Ways to Change the World
Without Leaving Your Cube

1. Defunk the Junk

   Stop junk mail. Unwanted junk mail wastes energy and trees.
   Signing up for a mail preference service can decrease the amount
   of mail you receive by up to seventy-five percent.

2. Re-gift

   Don't throw away old computers, electronics or office items.
   Instead, donate them to an agency that supports those in need.

3. I See the Light

   Use compact fluorescent lighting. Twenty percent of the electricity
   consumed in the U.S. is for lighting. Using compact fluorescent
   bulbs reduces energy.

4. Don't Use Virgins

   Buy recycled and create a market for recycled products. It is good
   for our world, our virgins and our jobs. Recycled paper requires
   twenty-three to seventy-four percent less energy to produce, which
   is important because the paper industry is the third largest energy

consumer in the U.S. Every ton of recycled paper substituted for nonrecycled paper also saves 380 gallons of oil and seventeen trees. Recycling a glass jar saves enough energy to light a hundred-watt lightbulb for four hours. You can make twenty cans from recycled material for the same amount of energy it takes to create one can made of virgin material. Incinerating ten thousand tons of waste creates one job, landfilling the same amount creates six jobs, recycling the same ten thousand tons creates *thirty-six jobs.*

5. Tech-Out

Don't print every draft. Review on your computer and use virtual storage rather than paper versions.

6. BYOC

Bring your own cup! Use a permanent water container and refill at the water cooler instead of using enough disposable cups to fill your living room twice. When you go out to lunch or to the coffee house, bring your own instead of wasting a cup whose lifespan is only the five minutes it took you to inhale your drink. Americans use 2,500,000 plastic bottles every hour, and most of them are never recycled!

7. Bagged!

Plastic bags and other plastic containers thrown into the ocean kill as many as one million sea creatures every year. When you go to the market or convenience store, bring your own canvas bag and save the world some plastic. Whole Foods and other conscientious markets offer a per-bag refund.

8. Join Bike Culture

Ride a bike, take public transportation or carpool with cuties to all your destinations. Remember to keep a correct amount of air in your auto tires—when they are low the car needlessly eats up more fuel.

9. Fair Play

As you fight for raises and fair pay at your work, promote those ideas elsewhere by buying products that are certified fair trade, which protects workers worldwide.

10. Out to Lunch

Be seafood smart. See if the fish you enjoy comes from a sustainable fishery to avoid overfishing, overexploiting our scarce resources.

Most figures obtained from the University of California, Berkeley, site, and we thank you!

The Gift

Give of yourself in an unexpected way this week. Take extra time to listen to someone's story, help a coworker after hours (particularly if he's cute), share a bit more of yourself, give. Receive. Give again.

The Gift, Part Deux

Write a wildly encouraging warrior motto on a piece of paper. Laminate it (ghetto lamination technique: Scotch tape, both sides). Keep it in your wallet for a month, give it to a ninja, ask her to "own" the motto for the next month, then ask her to re-gift, passing along the precept, the belief, the gift.

CHAPTER TWENTY-ONE: WARRIORS OF AN INCOGNITO KIND

One time when I was in high school, I was in this asylum-style emotional state, lost on my way to my dad's new apartment, which he had just moved into after my parents' perky-adorable divorce. I was astray, bright red, with tears streaming down my face, stopped in the middle of the street trying to figure out where to go. I looked over at some guy in a Volvo passing by and he simply lifted his hand, made a thumbs-up sign and gave me a smile that beamed, "Everything will be all right." It was so kind, so out of context, so minimal, and yet, like an arrow, it pierced straight through the feeling that I was riding it all alone. An act that took less than twenty seconds, still fresh in my mind *more than ten*

years later. There is something incredibly magical in random acts of kindness. In fact, whole bumper sticker cults are devoted to the suggestion of it.

The sage stage of giving is in doing so without words, without requirements, without pausing for thanks. This is the way of the warrior: not only to give, but to do so incognito. When it is anonymous it automatically circumvents all those messy human quirks like ego, wanting extra credit or buttering someone up for a requested return on a later date. When I was little and my brother wanted something I had, like my pink skateboard wheels, I would immediately go into bar-

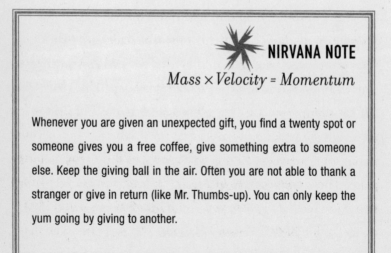

NIRVANA NOTE

Mass × Velocity = Momentum

Whenever you are given an unexpected gift, you find a twenty spot or someone gives you a free coffee, give something extra to someone else. Keep the giving ball in the air. Often you are not able to thank a stranger or give in return (like Mr. Thumbs-up). You can only keep the yum going by giving to another.

gaining mode: "I'll give you two wheels if you are nice to me for a week, four wheels for a month." As the youngest it was rare that someone wanted something I had, and rarer still that I could ever get people to play by my rules, so I used all I had to get all I thought I needed. Giving with expectations of return is like casting a line with a worm on a hook to reel in a fish, and then gutting the fish later. Bargaining in business is not only appropriate, it's intelligent, but in relationships with loved ones? Gutting. It sets up a spirit of power broker-ing and amputates the essence of true giving, which is love. Wanting the other to have more. Wanting the other to feel nice. Making life easier for someone you care about. Provid-ing new pink wheels so they can freely skate away. It can be difficult to do, but there is a litmus test if you are unsure of your gifting motives. Ask yourself before you give your free time, money or heart, "Will I resent this later? Will I be wait-ing for thanks, pausing for acknowledgment? Will I be irri-tated with a rash of 'Look at all I do for them'?" If you answer yes to any, then don't do it until you can do it from a pure place. There are two ways of giving: "Listen, I've got very lim-ited resources, if I give to you . . . it better be good and I bet-ter get a lot back." Versus, "Listen, cha cha, I've got mad amounts here, take some extra off my chops. Enjoy!" It's powerful to give from your pool of "enough." Plenty begets plenty; like mold, where some exists, more grows. One friend with incredible money karma claims that whenever she is financially insecure or tight, it is in that hour that she gives more, tips generously and is fluid with her money, kick-starting the flow. Like lowering national interest rates, which makes money easier to acquire, thus activating spending. It is because she sends the world a powerful message first, "I have more than enough," that the universe mirrors it back to her. It is just plain attractive and infectious. It is always then that money appears for her in forms of forgotten funds, surprise bonuses and tasty raises. Believe in abundance, live with a little thumbs-up and perform random acts of kindness, anonymously. You never know which simple little gift ends up profoundly affecting a perfect stranger, who may be silently grateful for years.

NIRVANA NOTES

Home Sweet Toxin-Free Recycled Energy-Efficient Green-Conscious Home!

1. Worms for Waste!

   In a lifetime, the average American will throw away six hundred times his or her adult weight in garbage. This means that we each will leave a legacy of ninety thousand pounds of trash for our children. Yard trimmings and food scraps make up about one-fourth of our waste. There are dozens of simple ways to compost from home, garden or even stuffy city studio. There's even a fun worm composting kit on the market that lets the worms do all the work.

2. One-Time Wonder

   Avoid buying one-time-use products, disposable razors, plastic harpoon applicators, overly packaged consumer products, and double-bagged movie videos (because Buddha forbid the movie *spills*). Buy rechargeable batteries, refillable razors, biodegradable or recyclable products. By recycling it is possible to cut our waste stream by eighty percent.

3. Breathe Clean

   According to EPA estimates, indoor air can be five times more polluted than the air outside. Volatile Organic Chemicals (VOCs) make up a portion of the air pollution that exists in homes from

common to respiratory problems and causes headaches, sinus congestion and fatigue. Certain plants soak up the VOCs, break them down and use them for food. Place two to three of the following house plants for every hundred square feet.

- Bamboo palm
- Lady palm
- Dwarf date palm
- Janet Craig dracaena
- English ivy
- Kimberly Queen
- Weeping fig
- Gerbera daisy
- Corn plant
- Warneckii dracaena

4. Kitty Conscious!

Clay cat litter produces a lot of dust, which contains silicon particles known as a human carcinogen. One study found that cats with respiratory disease had up to six times the amount of silica from clay-based litter as healthy cats. Look into other options, like pine—it's chemical-free, dust-free, biodegradable and does not cut any new trees for the product. Better yet, use shredded paper. Recycle, reuse! Harold can take a dookey on last month's bills and you can thank her for it.

5. Organic

Buying organic cuts down on pesticides and toxins in our world, and it reduces transportation emissions and packaging. And if you buy at farmers' markets you can actually meet and support the people feeding your family.

6. Think Green When You Clean

According to the Environmental Protection Agency, fifty percent of all illnesses can be traced to indoor air pollution caused by conventional household products. Most contain chemicals and toxins harmful to the environment—and to you! When they are dumped into sinks and landfills, hazardous chemical wastes can seep into groundwater, which nearly half of all Americans depend on for drinking water. Buy nontoxic cleaning supplies, many made available at healthful grocers like the Whole Foods Market.

7. Water Aware

Repair leaky faucets, as they can waste up to a hundred gallons of water per day. Buy water-conserving showerheads. Take showers with a partner to conserve water, and make sure he's adorable.

8. Corn Off the Cob

Each year, 352 million *pounds* of plastic are dumped into the sea. Plastic cups . . . bad. Paper cups consume trees, water and chemicals, and they are often wax-coated, which makes them non-recyclable. Paper cups . . . bad. Styrofoam . . . very bad. When throwing your next bbq, use the new line of corn-based biodegradable plastics, called polylactides or PLS. They degrade in forty-seven days, don't emit toxic fumes when incinerated and require twenty to fifty percent less fossil fuel to manufacture than regular plastics. Check companies like www.ecoproducts.com for these and other plastic product alternatives (trash bags, food containers). Also, make a habit of putting your money where your mouth is and refuse businesses that relentlessly use Styrofoam. Or give them info on these new products and bring your own cup!

9. Blinded by the Light

   Close blinds in summer to reduce need for electricity-binging AC, and open them in winter to reduce heating use.

10. Pulp Fiction

   Seventy-five thousand trees are used for the Sunday edition of the *New York Times* each week, yet only thirty percent of news-papers are recycled in the United States. Recycle, and make sure your favorite rags print on recycled paper. Another alternative: go pulp-free by reading online.

Most figures obtained from the University of California, Berkeley, site, and we thank you!

DOJO ON THE GO-GO

Miss Incognito

Ninjas, take up your arms . . . and then give with them! Each day for one entire week perform an anonymous act of giving. Walk a plate of food out to a street corner where hunger prevails. Drop a flower at the doorstep of a friend, or even better the doorstep of a foe; just don't get caught, 'cause that could just get strange. Leave a quarter in a stranger's parking meter that has run out; a "thank you, you are awfully cool" note on the napkin for your waiter. Then . . . don't tell anyone about your good deeds. See how exceedingly thumbs-up you feel at the end of the week.

CHAPTER TWENTY-TWO:
ENTER THE NINJA

Welcome, ninja chick: *you have arrived*. You delectable, adorable, pookey moose, chock-full of love! You have taken the six sacred precepts and you have emerged from your personal dojo of lessons *a ninja*. You have grown closer to Master Mama, that soft, inspiring, intuitive, wise voice inside that bellows out, "Are you mad, woman? Don't agree to go for drinks with *him*!" You are now a part of the secret society of warriors who are cheeky, in charge and simply genius; who live an unruly life of constant discovery. Who fly high and land well. Who speak the truth and stand right by it with strength. Who dig to the pit of the self, admit to the diamonds inside and believe in each and every one of them. Your mission now, should you choose to accept it, is to do nothing short of changing the world.

Now is the time to pass along what you've learned. It is in the teaching of concepts that they really coagulate within you. Like grappling with some new, complicated kung fu move, when you teach it to another, you finally get it yourself. In giving, we receive. Give others the gift of fewer broken bones by sharing in your bruised-up debacles. Give to others your precepts, your lessons. Invite others. Inspire others. Encourage others. Stir someone's day; stir someone's life. The greatest gift to our forest is not just our individual tree but what we leave, what we plant, what we grow. Give the seeds of revolution. Give the gift of the ninja!

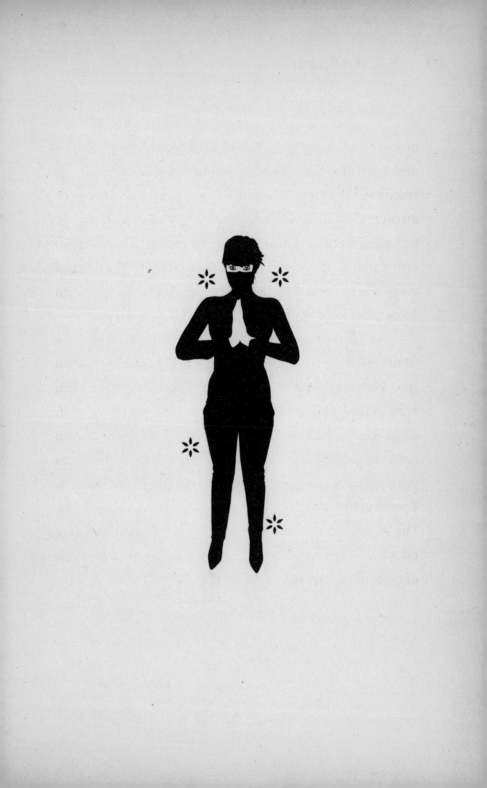

Photo by Siddhartha Abbazi

Born and raised in the landlocked state of Colorado, **Mollie Culligan** emigrated to Los Angeles, taught herself to surf, and founded an award-winning high-end jewelry and accessory line, the Jack Rabbit Collection.

Culligan is a lifelong activist, provocateur, and bacchante. *Ninja Chick* is her first book, thus far.